Growing Up
GREEN

Growing Up
GREEN

Problem-Based Investigations in Ecology and Sustainability for Young Learners in STEM

Stephen T. Schroth, Ph.D.,
& Janese Daniels, Ph.D.

Routledge
Taylor & Francis Group

NEW YORK AND LONDON

First published in 2021 by Prufrock Press Inc.

Published 2021 by Routledge
605 Third Avenue, New York, NY 10017
2 Park Square, Milton Park, Abingdon, Oxon OX14 4RN

Routledge is an imprint of the Taylor & Francis Group, an informa business

ISBN 13: 978-1-0321-4277-7 (hbk)
ISBN 13: 978-1-6463-2058-5 (pbk)

DOI: 10.4324/9781003235392

Table of Contents

Introduction

Environmental science provides an ideal opportunity for students of any age to build critical and creative thinking skills while also strengthening skills in science, technology, engineering, and mathematics (STEM). Exploring issues related to sustainability and environmental concerns helps students learn to identify problems, develop research questions, gather and analyze data, develop possible solutions, and disseminate this information to others. Green issues are appealing to today's learners because they are sensitive to the world around them and often long to engage in projects that touch on issues facing their communities. Although the relevance to STEM subjects is clear, green investigations can also build skills across the content areas, in diverse subjects such as English language arts, social studies, music, and art. A variety of resources, including the National Education for Sustainability (EfS) K–12 Learning Standards and the Common Core State Standards (CCSS), exist that can help educators create investigations for interested students.

Awareness of sustainability and environmental issues has grown rapidly in recent years, with many teachers and administrators attempting to add such instruction in their classrooms and schools (Cunningham & Saigo, 2001; Schroth, Helfer, LaRosa, et al., 2011; Spellman & Stoudt, 2013). Although all learners are interested in the environment, gifted students, especially, are often passionately concerned about the world around them and have a keen interest in work involv-

 DOI: 10.4324/9781003235392-1

ing issues that affect their lives (Renzulli & Reis, 2014; Treffinger et al., 2004). Parents and teachers can integrate sustainability education concepts into K–12 curriculum, thereby harnessing children's passion for green issues into projects and learning sequences that are robust, relevant, and rigorous (Spellman & Stoudt, 2013; Tomlinson, 2003; Treffinger et al., 2004). Projects that investigate sustainability and environmental concerns can touch upon all aspects of the curriculum, including English language arts, mathematics, social studies, science, art, music, and other areas (Johnson & Kendrick, 2005; Schroth, Helfer, Beck, & Swanson, 2011). Sustainability education is thus a high-interest field that also is adaptable to a variety of subjects (Cunningham & Saigo, 2001; Schroth, Helfer, LaRosa, et al., 2011; Spellman & Stoudt, 2013). Because investigations into sustainability and environmental issues can be both open-ended and complex, they are ideal areas of study for gifted learners (Renzulli & Reis, 2014; Schroth, 2007; Treffinger et al., 2004) but may appeal to learners of varying ability levels.

Many educators who want to explore sustainability and environmental issues with their young learners have certain questions, however:

- How can I integrate sustainability and environmental issues into my curriculum?
- What learning and content standards support sustainability education?
- Can I explore environmental issues with students at any age level?
- How can I permit students to investigate problems they have identified while still adhering to certain learning objectives?
- Are there resources that can assist me in adapting a green curriculum?

Happily, there are a variety of ways to integrate sustainability education concepts at any level of the K–12 curriculum, either as stand-alone activities or as a discrete area of study (Renzulli & Reis, 2014; Schroth, Helfer, LaRosa, et al., 2011; Tomlinson et al., 2009; Treffinger et al., 2004). *Growing Up Green*'s guided investigations examine methods of instruction that assist in shaping investigations about environmental issues, ways to differentiate instruction to meet learners' needs, and examples of projects that can be used in early childhood settings (grades K–2).

The investigations can be used in general education classrooms, in single- or multigrade gifted classrooms, or as part of a pull-out program. The investigations are designed to offer a week's worth of instruction and activities—we have also made each subpart of the guided investigations an independent and autonomous stand-alone instructional sequence. For those who have limited time and resources to devote to environmental science, you may select a handful of these sequences to provide your students with rich and relevant experiences with the subjects covered. It goes without saying, but this book can be used with a variety of other instructional programs and approaches, serving either as an independent way of working with STEM topics or as a supplement to existing plans. Time-tested programs such as Junior Great Books or Creative Problem Solving would work terrifically with the materials presented here (Treffinger et al., 2006). This book presents 10 separate guided investigations, each divided into individual inquiry sequences (activities). Additionally, a variety of resources, including the National Education for Sustainability K–12 Student Learning Standards and the Common Core State Standards that support sustainability education, electronic resources such as apps and websites, children's literature, and other instructional materials that support such learning, will be referenced throughout the guided investigations and are included in appendices at the end of the book. The end of the book also includes a standards alignment chart that details the CCSS for each investigation.

Getting Started With Guided Investigations

A brief explanation of what guided investigations are, how to implement them in a classroom, and ways to use them with either the whole class or in small groups of students may be helpful. Children make sense of their world by synthesizing new experiences into what they have come to understand. Essentially, students approach new information, sort through it, compare it with what they have learned before, and ultimately adjust this new insight so that it fits in with their worldview. Teachers can support this process by using primary resources, encouraging student autonomy, using open-ended questions, and seeking elaboration of students' answers.

The goal with guided investigations is to build students' retention, understanding, and active use of knowledge. *Retention* involves the acquisition of organized information in the mind, as well as the ability to recall that knowledge when appropriate. *Understanding* affects the development of intellectual skills and processes, the means of using the knowledge that is learned or recalled. *Active use of knowledge* establishes understanding of ideas and values, permitting students to make them their own.

Attaining these goals occurs only when all players—including students, parents, teachers, and administrators—see "conspicuous gains" at "minimally increased cost" (Perkins, 1992, p. 164). In other words, everyone wants to see lots of achievement bang for their instructional bucks. Rather than emphasizing the memorization of facts, teachers must focus on helping students to acquire the data pertinent to given problems as they arise. Students must be provided with rich and authentic problems and challenges that require the use and manipulation of knowledge to forge a solution (Brisk & Harrington, 2007). As educators help students acquire certain characteristics and qualities that predict success in later life—mindfulness, resilience, grit and the like—they must structure instructional sequences that provide students with opportunities to use creative and critical thinking skills by devising solutions to open-ended problems that do not have a single resolution.

A project-based approach in the classroom, such as guided investigations, permits young learners to experience active, engaged, and relevant learning (Helm & Katz, 2011). Project-based learning is centered on the learner and presents them with the prospect of an in-depth investigation of valuable and worthwhile topics (Bruner, 1966; Smutny, 2016). The goal is to create autonomous learners who are able to construct personally meaningful products and artifacts that embody their learning from the process (Isaksen et al., 2011; Smutny & von Fremd, 2010). Guided investigations provide opportunities for children to express their curiosity in a purposeful manner and experience, sometimes for the first time, the joy of self-motivated learning (Helm & Katz, 2011; Schroth, 2018). When you use a well-developed guided investigation, you will engage students' minds and emotions, fostering a love of learning and levels of engagement that are rare in many classrooms (Schroth et al., 2019; Treffinger et al., 2004).

Today's learners are more diverse than ever before—students with learning challenges, gifted students, English language learners, students from low-income backgrounds, and other groups (Schroth & Helfer, 2018; Tomlinson, 2014). The incidence of single-parent households and children who are English language learners has increased exponentially. Parents, who work more hours than ever before, do not have the time and, in some cases, the skills to support their child's learning at home. Traditional recreational endeavors such as reading and athletics, which supported the school's academic programming, have been supplanted by video games, smartphones, and other such activities. All of this has resulted in more and more diversity.

Students learn best when the work they do in school is relevant to their lives and their communities. For instruction to take root, children must thus investigate real-life problems that touch upon and affect their world. Such problems, with open-ended solutions, will intrigue and interest young learners, spurring their best efforts and the most complete engagement possible. Teachers play an active role in guiding each child's progress. Students embarking on guided investigations require superb teaching, as their misconceptions and immature thinking demand careful guidance. While leading a guided investigation, teachers will balance issues and disciplines and language to assure maximum learning (Adler, 1984; Schroth, 2007).

Students learn best when they are provided with a moderate challenge (Tomlinson, 2014). When instructional tasks are much too difficult for a learner, they feel threatened and, as a means of self-protection, may not persist with thinking or problem solving (Tomlinson, 2003). Conversely, tasks that are too simple also suppress a learner's thinking and problem-solving processes—rather than learning, a child presented with work that is too easy drifts through school, unchallenged by and indifferent to the learning process (Tomlinson, 2014). Schools and classrooms seek to differentiate instruction as much as possible so that the needs of all learners are met (Tomlinson, 2014). Teachers can improve the success of differentiated instruction in their classroom by organizing resources to support change.

Although in some ways differentiated instruction is so appealing because it simply represents good teaching, we acknowledge that many educators struggle to implement it with integrity in the classroom. When well done, differentiated instruction is deep, profound, and multifaceted, and benefits all children in the classroom. Differentiated instruction recognizes and honors children's varying skills and needs, providing them with a learning environment in which they are included, respected, and provided with an appropriate level of challenge. If you are a novice teacher, differentiation provides a configuration you can use to establish your practice, and if you are a seasoned veteran of the classroom it continues to demand adjustment and improvement of delivery and performance. Differentiation at its core asks teachers to determine the readiness, interests, and learning needs of each student, and then to provide each student with activities and instruction that are appropriate, beneficial, and coherent.

In assessing student learning and interacting with your class, you should determine students' readiness levels, interests, and learning profiles (see Figure 1). *Readiness* refers to the knowledge, understanding, and skills related to the content covered in a particular instructional sequence, which may relate to achievement but also to prior experiences. *Interest* concerns those events and subjects that spur students' curiosity and evoke their passions. *Learning profiles* relate to learning styles, intelligence preferences, culture, gender, and other such attributes. Using knowledge of these three traits, you may alter the process, product, or learning environment in which you will have students work. *Process* involves those activities and practices you will have learners engage in to make sense of information, ideas, and skills. *Product* entails how students will demonstrate what they know, understand, and are able to do as a result of the instructional sequence. *Learning environment* is concerned with the operation, tone, and atmosphere of the learning space. You will change and adjust these to deal with student differences.

Throughout these investigations, emphasis will be placed on how to differentiate activities so that they best meet the needs of gifted learners and support

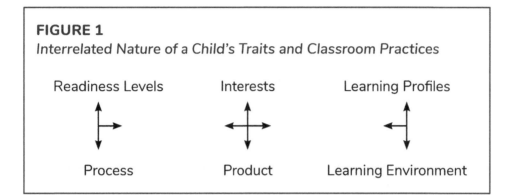

FIGURE 1

Interrelated Nature of a Child's Traits and Classroom Practices

Readiness Levels	Interests	Learning Profiles
Process	Product	Learning Environment

their strengths. Changing assignments, altering groups, or switching how content is provided will be done as needed to provide the optimal learning situation for the children with whom you work.

Taking Inventory of Our Resources

Creating an Environmental Impact Statement

AN environmentally responsible community maintains its existing natural resources in addition to trying to make positive and proactive change. In many communities, a development or construction project must be approved before it can take place. One factor that helps determine whether or not the project may begin is a determination that the proposed construction will leave the area in as good of or better condition than it was before the project began. For such a determination to take place, communities must know the status of various areas in their current state, which would include the number of trees present on given parcels of land.

In this investigation, students will prepare an environmental impact statement (EIS) to help determine the fate of a proposed project. An EIS is a tool used for decision making by government agencies and legislative bodies. A strong EIS will describe both the positive and negative environmental effects of a proposed action and help decision makers to fully understand the situation at hand. An EIS often will also list one or more alternative solutions.

Students will prepare an EIS related to a development, real or imagined, that will affect their community. A part of the EIS will be comprised of a chart that shows how many trees, and of what type, currently exist on a given piece of prop-

DOI: 10.4324/9781003235392-2

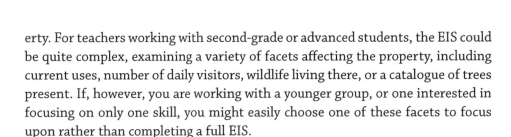

erty. For teachers working with second-grade or advanced students, the EIS could be quite complex, examining a variety of facets affecting the property, including current uses, number of daily visitors, wildlife living there, or a catalogue of trees present. If, however, you are working with a younger group, or one interested in focusing on only one skill, you might easily choose one of these facets to focus upon rather than completing a full EIS.

Assessing Prior Learning

For a pretest activity, ask students to prepare a bar graph of how children in the class got to school that day. Did they walk to school . . . come by the school bus . . . get dropped off from their parents' automobile? Quickly assess these bar graphs for accuracy and grasp of the concept, and then record this information.

Planning and Teaching

Participants/Grouping: Students may be grouped using a variety of strategies. A mixed-ability classroom teacher might group students by readiness levels, placing them with two or three other students with similar experiences and abilities, and then provide each group with the appropriate amount of scaffolding and support according to their skills and needs. Students may also be grouped according to their interests, which allows each group to attack individual parts of the EIS. The various small-group contributions can then be combined in a manner that would permit the class as a whole to produce a single EIS.

Standards: EfS Standard 2.2; CCSS.ELA-LITERACY.CCRA.W.7

8

ACTIVITY 1.1
Tree Hunt

Objective

Students will engage in a tree hunt, finding trees with different qualities, recording their findings, and sharing them with others using written, electronic, or other means.

Modifications

Group students by readiness levels into groups of two or three. Lower readiness levels can group trees as "big," "small," and the like, while more advanced students can classify them as "conifers," "deciduous," or other appropriate distinctions. Older or higher ability students may further identify trees by using their common names, their scientific names, or both (e.g., white spruce, *Picea glauca*).

Materials

- Teacher's copy of Jason Chin's *Redwoods*
- Clipboard or whiteboard for each student
- Paper, pencils, markers, colored pencils, construction paper, glue sticks, scissors, and other materials necessary for students to write and create
- Student access to computers, tablets, phones, or other electronic devices with Internet access (optional)

Instructional Sequence

Introduction and Motivation: Read Jason Chin's *Redwoods* to the class and discuss how trees may appear to be different or the same, charting student responses.

ACTIVITY 1.1, *continued*

Procedures:

1. Help students conceptualize how to take an inventory and why one might engage in this process. Think aloud about how students might categorize trees they view, using a pictorial representation projected on a SMART Board or other device.

2. Mention different attributes one might use to compare and contrast, and then show students how they might record this information, using lists, tally marks, pictograms, or other symbols to do so.

3. Distribute clipboards or individual whiteboards and let groups practice recording information using another pictorial representation.

4. Take students on a walking field trip or to a nearby park so that each group may record its data.

5. Have students use tools of their choice to represent their data to others. Appropriate ways of representing these data might include bar charts made with construction paper, computer-generated charts from a spreadsheet, or news shared using social media, such as via a class Twitter, Instagram, TikTok, or Facebook page.

Closure: Have students share their results with others via a gallery walk to which other classes, families, and administrators are invited.

Assessment: Assess student representations of their bar graphs using a rubric/criteria chart previously created with the class. This criteria chart, which will help students understand when their work is completed, might require students to list each type of tree observed, either by picture or name, and include tally marks next to each type of tree indicating the number seen. More advanced learners might also use the Green Map System website (https://www.greenmap.org), which permits the creation of digital community maps, to document their findings.

Evaluation: Document evidence of learning at the individual and group level, explaining the results of students who learned more or less than expected. Discuss these results with students in individual meetings.

Reflection: Consider this experience in terms of your performance, examining if reteaching is necessary and what changes in teaching might improve the results.

ACTIVITY 1.2
Property Uses

Objective

Students will determine current uses of property, including uses that might not be evident from deeds and government records, recording their findings and sharing these with others using written, electronic, or other means.

Modifications

Group students by readiness levels into groups of two or three. Lower readiness levels might examine how a property is used based upon observed use of the property during business hours, while more advanced students can investigate government records, interview neighbors of the property, and/or set up webcams (with permission) to determine after-hour usage. Older and high-ability students may further discuss ways the property might be used with experts, who might include any of the following: an architect, a landscape architect, a builder, a construction company worker, a city or town alderman or alderwoman, a mayor, a county supervisor, a land-use planning commission member, a parks commission member, a youth recreation leader, or a zoning board member.

Materials

- Teacher's copy of Bao Phi's *A Different Pond*
- Paper, pencils, markers, colored pencils, construction paper, glue sticks, scissors, and other materials necessary for students to write and create
- Student access to computers, tablets, phones, or other electronic devices with Internet access
- An online tool that permits the publication of student work, such as:
  - Penzu, a customizable online journal (https://penzu.com)
  - Flipsnack, a tool to create, embed, and share online magazines (https://www.flipsnack.com)

ACTIVITY 1.2, *continued*

- WordPress, a popular webpage builder (https://wordpress.com)
- Lulu, an online ePub or PDF book platform (https://www.lulu.com/create/ebooks)

Instructional Sequence

Introduction and Motivation: Read Bao Phi's *A Different Pond* to the class, discussing how the same plot of land may be used differently by different people. Emphasize how the significance of a piece of land might not be visible, as in the case where it reminds users of their homeland.

Procedures:

1. Help students focus on what use of a piece of property entails by asking students to brainstorm various ways in which their school is used. Anticipated responses from students could include teaching and learning, but they might also touch upon the various other uses of the building, such as its use as a place for eating breakfast and lunch, as a library, as a community center, as a place for athletics, as a theater, etc.

2. Ask students how they think previous generations of students might remember or view the school (if applicable).

3. Then, ask students how they might be able to find out about the uses of a property they do not use on a daily basis. Anticipated responses might include observing the property, asking people who use the property, asking neighbors of the property, searching government records, and asking experts in land use and development.

4. Next, have students investigate a given property with a partner or partners and record their information. The property investigated might be a vacant lot, a housing development, a shopping center, a leisure or recreation area, or any such commonly found use of land. Appropriate ways of representing this information might include pie charts made with construction paper, narrative explanations with photographs of the property, podcasts or other recordings of interviews, video interviews, or interactive maps.

Closure: Have students share their results with others in small groups, where they will receive feedback about the strengths of their summaries as well as suggestions for changes they might make to help others better understand their findings.

ACTIVITY 1.2, *continued*

Assessment: Have students use one of several available tools to publish their findings. Some of the more useful publishing tools available for no fee are included in the Materials section of this investigation. Assess student representations using a rubric/criteria chart previously created with the class. This criteria chart, which will help students understand when their work is completed, might require students to (a) describe the property that is examined, including as many details as possible, such as neighborhood, address, name of the property, and the like; (b) include photographs of the property, drawings, and diagrams showing how the property is used; (c) list information they have found out about prior uses of the property; and (d) use one of the programs or apps listed in the Materials section to publish their work.

Evaluation: Document evidence of learning at the individual and group level, explaining the results of students who learned more or less than expected. Discuss these results with students in individual meetings.

Reflection: Consider this experience in terms of your performance, especially as related to the discussions you led regarding *A Different Pond*, and how effective this was in permitting students to understand how a piece of property might have uses and value that cannot be seen by the casual observer but only understood through talking with users of that property. As a result of this examination, determine if reteaching is necessary and what changes in teaching might improve the results.

ACTIVITY 1.3
Wildlife and Human Property

Objective

Students will consider how wildlife, such as birds, animals, and fish, use a given piece of property. Special consideration will be given to how the wildlife interact and live with humans. Students will not need to make a determination of the quality of these interactions, nor come up with possible solutions to the problem of how humans and other wildlife can best coexist on a particular piece of property. (If such determinations or solutions are desired, ask students to come up with these; doing this might prove especially beneficial for high-ability students.)

Modifications

Group students by interests into groups of two or three. Those with an affinity for birds might be grouped together, those who like mammals in another group, and so forth.

Materials

- Teacher's copy of Matthew Cordell's *Wolf in the Snow*
- A map of the local community, which may be either a paper map or online map via Google Maps, Bing Maps, or OpenStreetMap
- Graph paper or blank paper for each student
- Scratch paper and clipboard for each student
- Student access to computers, tablets, phones, or other electronic devices with Internet access (optional)

Instructional Sequence

Introduction and Motivation: Read Matthew Cordell's *Wolf in the Snow*, a mostly wordless book that details the encounter between a little girl and a wolf cub, both of whom are lost in a snowstorm.

ACTIVITY 1.3, *continued*

Procedures:

1. Discuss how *Wolf in the Snow* shows both humans and wildlife sharing the same environment. Concentrate the discussion on discerning similarities and differences in the use of the land by the little girl and the wolf.

2. Demonstrate how to create a map, using the classroom itself as an example, and then show the class how to use similar skills to craft a map of the property being studied.

3. Take students on a walking field trip to a piece of property where wildlife lives or uses the area. Bring along a clipboard and scratch paper for each student. Find a place where the class can sit or stand silently, and then observe the property for 20 or 30 minutes. Have students watch for various animals (e.g., squirrels, foxes, birds, etc.), and have them record the animal they observed, how many times it was observed, and (for older children) what the animal was doing.

4. Using skills gained during the process of tracking use of the property (i.e., observation, using tally marks to record the number of animals observed, using minicams to track animals using the property at night, etc.), students should use icons to represent wildlife using the property on a map. Depending on the available technology, groups might use the Green Map System (https://www.greenmap.org) to create maps that show the wildlife living on the property.

Closure: Have groups create a natural history museum, where they will display their maps of the area and discuss living creatures that use the property.

Assessment: Assess student representations of wildlife living on or using the property using a rubric previously created with the class. If students use the Green Map System website, assess their use of that as well.

Evaluation: Document evidence of learning at the individual and group level, explaining the results of students who learned more or less than expected. Discuss these results with students in individual meetings.

Reflection: Consider this experience in terms of your performance, examining if reteaching is necessary and what changes in teaching might improve the results.

ACTIVITY 1.4
Writing an Environmental Impact Statement

Objective

Students will prepare and publish an environmental impact statement (EIS), using their output from the three previous investigations. Alternatively, the class may produce one EIS that can then be shared with others.

Modifications

Group students by learning profile to work on assembling an EIS. This means that some students might prefer to work alone, while others might prefer being a member of a small group of two or three. Each student or group will assemble an EIS based upon the work each did in their previous groups. This should provide students working with others several options for each portion of the EIS. If you elect to create a class EIS, have students vote to select the representative artifact for each section of the document.

Materials

- A sample copy of an environmental impact study, such as those available here:
  - https://www.iisd.org/learning/eia/examples
  - https://cdn.friendsoftheearth.uk/sites/default/files/downloads/EIA%20campaigners%20guide.pdf
  - https://www.boem.gov/environment/environmental-assessment/environmental-impact-statement-eis-format-and-content-process

- Student access to computers, tablets, phones, or other electronic devices with Internet access and word processing software
- A list of those items you want included in the EIS. These may include:
  - A title page, including names of group members and the date
  - Table of contents

- A signature page for all authors of the EIS
- A description of the site location, including address, photographs, and the like
- A map or diagram of the property
- A list of all vegetation and wildlife observed on the property
- Observed uses of the property by wildlife and humans
- Conclusions and recommendations

Instructional Sequence

Introduction and Motivation: Show students an EIS that has been prepared as the result of a request to develop a parcel of land (see the examples in the Materials list). Explain that this document is used by town councils, boards, and other legislative bodies to determine whether or not the proposed development will help or harm the local environment, and whether or not to let the development proceed. Tell students that they will prepare an EIS for the parcel of land they have been studying, and then share this with the community in which they live.

Procedures:

1. Explain that an EIS must be organized in a way that makes it accessible and easy for those reading it to find relevant information. Go through the sample EIS, perhaps using a document camera, to show the class how an EIS is organized.

2. Share with students the sections that their EISs should contain, such as an introduction, an inventory of trees on the property, a list of current uses of the property, a list of animals that use the property, etc. See the Materials list for more guidance. Provide a visual representation of these sections that students may use as a model.

3. Divide students into groups (if desired) and have each student or group construct their own EIS.

4. Once the class EIS (or the various student and group EISs) are complete, decide how to share the document with an authentic audience.
   - If a single class EIS is produced, students may elect to send it to their city or town council representative, either by letter or at an in-person meeting.

ACTIVITY 1.4, *continued*

- If individual students and small groups produce their own EISs, they may elect to share these with administrators, parents, and other classes.

Closure: Have students share their results with others via an open house to which other classes, families, and administrators are invited.

Assessment: Assess students' EISs using a rubric previously created with the class. Depending upon the time available for the investigation, you may also elect to assess how students have disseminated the EIS, looking at letters they may have drafted to local leaders or how they set up their displays and then explained these at the open house. The individual portions of the EISs, with the exception of the introduction and the recommendations, have been previously evaluated, so you will not have to examine these in providing a final assessment of the investigation.

Evaluation: Document evidence of students' learning at the individual and group level, explaining the results of students who learned more or less than expected. With this final step, show special interest in each student's understanding of why an EIS may be required and how its production affects the proposed development. Discuss these results with students in individual meetings.

Reflection: Consider this experience in terms of your performance, examining if reteaching is necessary and what changes in teaching might improve the results.

Advocating for Change

Interacting With Government Decision Makers

THOSE advocating for increased parkland, new development, restrictions on land use, or programs supporting sustainable behavior must identify, interact with, and influence government decision makers. This investigation will explore how to do this in order to advance an environmental initiative.

The best investigations stem from actual problems facing the communities in which students live, so work with students to identify an issue that involves land use within their neighborhood. At times, this issue will disclose itself naturally, such as when a student asks, "Why are there no bike trails in our community?" or "Why is our school playground older and less attractive than another school's?" Sometimes, however, you will need to brainstorm with students to identify an issue or challenge facing their community.

Brainstorming may be done as part of a small-group exercise, although most times it will work best in a whole-group setting. Read to the class *Maybe Something Beautiful: How Art Transformed a Neighborhood* by F. Isabel Campoy and Theresa Howell. This fictional work was inspired by the efforts of Rafael López, who created the Urban Art Trail in San Diego's East Village. The protagonist of *Maybe Something Beautiful*, Mira, is a girl who loves to draw, doodle, paint, and

 DOI: 10.4324/9781003235392-3

create. She is saddened by the austerity of her urban neighborhood and seeks to transform her neighborhood through the creation of murals. The book documents the process she went through and provides illustrations and photographs of the jewel-toned murals that enlivened the East Village neighborhood.

Reading this story will provide the class with a foundation of knowledge about how individuals may affect positive change on the environment around them. It will also activate students' prior knowledge and provide them with opportunities to see a kid of a similar age look at the world around her, make a determination of something that could be improved, and then take positive steps to make changes that address an issue. Think aloud at various points when reading the book, and interject comments such as, "Mira has noticed that her neighborhood is made up mainly of blank walls, benches, and utility boxes," "Mira decides that she wants her community to be more beautiful," and "Mira thought about those things she is good at and remembered that she loves to draw, doodle, and paint." Connections between things seen in *Maybe Something Beautiful* and the school neighborhood, if appropriate, might also be made.

Assessing Prior Learning

After reading *Maybe Something Beautiful* with the class, check if students understood that the community was transformed through the work of Mira and her peers. This can be determined through a class discussion or using a beginning/middle/end chart, where students draw a caption showing something that happened at the beginning, in the middle, or at the end of the story.

Planning and Teaching

Participants/Grouping: For this investigation, students may again be grouped using a variety of strategies. A variety of whole-group, small-group, and individual instruction may be used. Grouping decisions may be made based upon students' readiness levels, interests, or learning profiles. For example, if a group of students is interested in developing a bike path, and another group is interested in establishing a series of murals on school and other community building walls, students can be grouped along these lines, with diverse readiness levels in each group. Similarly, if one group of students are proficient or advanced writers, while the others are still at the beginning level, one group might work on writing letters to city aldermen, legislators, and other decision makers, while the other groups may concentrate on crafting posters supporting their viewpoint. Finally, groupings might be determined by students' preferred learning style. Depending upon the objectives, students may choose to work alone, with a partner, or in a small group of their choosing. Conversely, if you are trying to build students' social skills, you might elect to place them in groups of your choosing.

Standards: EfS Standards 3.1, 3.2; CCSS.ELA-LITERACY.CCRA.W.2; CCSS.MATH.CONTENT.1.NBT

ACTIVITY 2.1
Implementing Change

Objective

Students will determine a change they want made in their communities, develop a plan for the implementation of this change, and communicate with elected officials who might assist in making this change occur through letters and other written communications.

Modifications

At the center of this guided investigation are the intertwined skills of identifying something that needs changing and then advocating for that change with the appropriate decision makers. By the end of first grade, many students will be able to take on these tasks independently, but interaction with others can improve the content of the work of even the most able student. If you have students who you believe might be unable to complete the writing required of a letter or advocacy piece, these students might be grouped with others and assigned tasks, such as finding exemplars of their intended project online or drawing or assembling illustrations to support the effort.

Materials

- Teacher's copy of Susan Verde's *The Water Princess*
- Chart paper, whiteboard, SMART Board, or other way to record student responses and display them
- Photographs of some of the buildings where decision makers in your community work, such as photos of city hall, the county courthouse/building, the school district central office, or other similar locations
- Poster board, construction paper, markers, crayons, scissors, glue sticks, and other materials needed to make a display
- A list of words useful in politely asking for something, such as: *please, could you?, consider, we respectfully request, would it be possible?, would appreciate it if, would be grateful if, kindly, thank you*

ACTIVITY 2.1, *continued*

Instructional Sequence

Introduction and Motivation: Read Susan Verde's *The Water Princess* (illustrated by Peter H. Reynolds) to the class. The book relates the life experiences of Georgie Badiel, a Burkina Faso-born high fashion model who is also the founder of the Georgie Badiel Foundation, an entity that works to provide access to clean drinking water to people living around the globe. The book relays the story of Princess Gie Gie, a young girl who helps her mother each day by journeying alongside her to bring water back to their home for use in cooking and cleaning. Although the daily task is joyful and pleasant for Princess Gie Gie, it is also time-consuming and arduous, and the daily hardships of such a journey are also acknowledged. Students will enjoy the beautiful yet simple representations of West Africa, and the character of Princess Gie Gie is both sympathetic and relatable. The book provides excellent information about the global water crisis and the need for collaboration to address problems facing us collectively.

Procedures:

1. Think aloud about how the community in which Princess Gie Gie lives struggles with a task necessary for their health and well-being.

2. Encourage students to develop a list of reasons Princess Gie Gie, her mother, and others need water, including drinking it, cooking with it, bathing in it, and cleaning with it. If possible, this list should be generated by students in response to a question, such as "How do we use water every day?"

3. Brainstorm ways people can ask for something to be changed, such as asking the city council to change the time of waste collection at your home or a group of children asking their school principal to begin a recycling program.

4. Have students develop a list of ways the people in Princess Gie Gie's community might advocate for better access to water. They may work individually or with a partner, but they should each compile a list of several ways that people might improve their access to quality water.

5. Have students share some of the ways that Princess Gie Gie's community might advocate for better access to water.

ACTIVITY 2.1, *continued*

Closure: Ask students to create posters that show various ways one might advocate for change, including methods such as telephoning, writing a letter/email, creating an organization, or protesting.

Assessment: Assess students' understanding of how one might advocate for a position or perspective by examining the lists they generated and the posters they created.

Evaluation: Consider evidence of learning at the individual and group level. Think especially about those students who demonstrated greater or less learning than you had expected. Discuss the results of this analysis with the class.

Reflection: Consider this experience in terms of your performance, paying special attention to students' understanding of the vocabulary used in *The Water Princess*. Did students seem comfortable with the vocabulary? Were there any words that students did not seem to know? How do you know this? Consider if the answers to these questions require any adjustments in your teaching as you continue this guided investigation.

ACTIVITY 2.2
Environmental Impact

Objective

Students will understand how the actions of individuals can improve the health of the environment. Special emphasis will be placed on how one's actions and choices result in the degradation or improvement of the environment, and that by choosing the deed that has the least negative or most positive impact, one can collectively make a great difference.

Modifications

Most students in the class will have little trouble counting the plastic bags they personally collect, but as the class begins to combine the group's bags, the larger numbers will present difficulties for those struggling with place value. Rather than focusing upon the total number of bags collected, students might instead concentrate on the number of sets of 10 assembled.

Materials

- Student copies of Handout 2.2: Keeping Track of Plastic Bags
- Teacher's copy of Miranda Paul's One *Plastic Bag: Isatou Ceesay and the Recycling Women of the Gambia*
- Several disposable plastic grocery bags
- Pencils, markers, paper, mini whiteboards, and other ways for students to record information
- Chart paper, construction paper, rulers, stamps, and other materials needed to create a display of students' findings.

Instructional Sequence

Introduction and Motivation: Read One *Plastic Bag: Isatou Ceesay and the Recycling Women of the Gambia* to the class. This book examines how a group of Gambian women addressed the problem generated by hundreds of disposable plastic bags that had accumulated by the side of the

ACTIVITY 2.2, *continued*

road, allowing water to pool in them, which in turn brought mosquitoes and disease.

Procedures:

1. Discuss the various problems caused by plastic bags. Students should understand that although inexpensive and handy to carry items, the plastic bags caused disease, killed goats and other animals that ate them, and strangled gardens when attempts to bury the excess bags were tried. Isatou Ceesay's efforts to collect the bags and repurpose them into other items eliminated the problem caused by the bags and created an industry that employs many and provides them with income.

2. Next, exhibit some disposable plastic bags that you have accumulated through a week of shopping—discuss how this number, multiplied by the number of students in the class, shows the approximate number of bags generated by the class during a week.

3. Show the class that there are different ways of representing this number. You can display it as a numeral, or you can represent it as a series of tally marks or other symbols that represent a certain number.

4. Provide students with a template for keeping track of plastic bags (see Handout 2.2: Keeping Track of Plastic Bags) and show them various ways one can keep track of a number up to 100, including using numerals, tally marks, and symbols.

5. Ask students to bring in plastic bags that their families use during the week. Count these with the class each day, and let students work independently or in groups to count and record the number of plastic bags collected.

6. Ask students to generate ideas that might reduce the number of plastic bags the class collectively uses each week. Ways to reduce this number might include recycling the bags, using cloth bags rather than taking plastic bags from the store, and for small loads, refusing a bag altogether.

Closure: Have students create large representations of the number of bags collected during the week, using numerals, tally marks, or symbols.

ACTIVITY 2.2, *continued*

Assessment: Review student answers to discussion questions and collect their efforts to record the number of plastic bags collected each day and at the end of the week. For those who struggle with counting, you may elect to work with them in a small group to reinforce these skills.

Evaluation: Consider student demonstrations of mastery or struggles at the individual and group level. More advanced learners may be ready to progress to multiplication, while those who face considerable challenges may benefit from more hands-on experiences.

Reflection: As you look back on this sequence of instructional activities, consider what went well, what was unexpected, and what you would do differently if taught again. Also think about what the next steps of instruction should be for this group.

Name: _____ Date: _____

Keeping Track of Plastic Bags

Directions: Use this template keep track of plastic bags that you find or see during the week. Each time you see a plastic bag, put a tally mark in one of the boxes, until you get to 10. At that point, start in the next box.

ACTIVITY 2.3
Using Words for Social Change

Objective

Students will explore how the written word can be used to advocate for considerable social change. Forms of written word will include letters, posters, and books.

Modifications

Depending upon the number of products you want generated as a result of this investigation, students may be grouped as a whole class or into smaller groups, or work alone. If one product is desired from the whole class, you might choose to compose a class book on a single theme, which will have individual pages or chapters comprised by individuals or smaller groups. If a poster or letter is desired, students can work individually or in pairs to produce a poster or letter advocating for a certain position.

Materials

- Student copies of Handout 2.3: Storyboard
- Teacher's copy of Laurie Lawlor's *Rachel Carson and Her Book That Changed the World*
- Teacher's copies of *The Sea Around Us* and *Silent Spring* by Rachel Carson (optional)
- Chart paper, whiteboard, SMART Board, or other way to record student responses and display them
- Paper, pencils, markers, colored pencils, construction paper, glue sticks, scissors, and other materials necessary for students to write and create
- Rulers, stamps, ink pad, construction paper, yarn, colored pipe cleaners, and other materials that can be used for decoration
- Student access to computers, tablets, phones, or other electronic devices with Internet access

Instructional Sequence

Introduction and Motivation: Read Laurie Lawlor's *Rachel Carson and Her Book That Changed the World* to the class. This book explores how Rachel Carson overcame societal indifference and antipathy to environmental concerns, and the sexism prevalent during the first half of the 20th century, to write a number of books that are credited today with beginning the global environmental movement, including *The Sea Around Us* (winner of a United States National Book Award) and *Silent Spring*, the book referred to in Lawlor's title.

Procedures:

1. Help students think about how writing can be used for advocacy. Ask students if they can recall a time that they or their parents tried to change something, and then ask them to elaborate by mentioning how they went about doing this. Anticipated replies might include, "I took a toy I received as a gift back to a store and returned it at the customer service counter," or "My mother wasn't happy with the tickets we received at the movie theater and asked to speak with the manager," or "My dad didn't like a new law so he wrote a letter to our legislator." If examples of this type prove difficult to elicit, you might provide some yourself.

2. Brainstorm as a class and develop a list of environmental concerns facing the local school community—these might include items such as better playground equipment, eliminating the use of trays in the lunchroom to save water (or, if some disposable material, reducing waste), or encouraging students, faculty, and staff to take public transportation to school.

3. Discuss how students might best express these views. Assuming the goal is to promote better playground equipment, the class might decide to take Rachel Carson's lead and write a book advocating for this. The book might comprise a series of chapters, each focusing upon a different aspect of the issue, such as:
   - the value of exercise,
   - types of exercise that are especially beneficial,
   - how playground equipment supports exercise,
   - the state of the school's current playground equipment, and
   - how new playground equipment would foster more exercise and thus better health.

ACTIVITY 2.3, *continued*

4. Assign students to small groups to work on the chapters. Before having them work independently, discuss the parameters for students' work. These might include:
    -   each chapter must have a minimum of 8 pages,
    -   each page must contain an illustration and some text,
    -   each chapter must first have a storyboard that details how the chapter will proceed before students start working on the pages (see Handout 2.3: Storyboard), and
    -   all members of the group must contribute an illustration and one page of text for the chapter (the chapter may be dictated if needed, depending on students' ability levels).

5. Monitor students' work, moving from group to group to ensure that each is on task and proceeding toward a product that fulfills the model set forth in *Rachel Carson and Her Book That Changed the World*.

Closure: After the chapters are finished, combine them into a book. Host a book launch party—a celebratory event with other classes, administrators, and parents invited to attend.

Assessment: Assess students' work using the storyboard assignment as well as the completed chapters themselves. Of these, the storyboards are perhaps the most important, as they will help you determine how well students are attaining your goals and permit you time to regroup, reteach, and revise work that is not headed in the way you intended.

Evaluation: Document evidence of learning on an individual, small-group, and whole-group basis, using photographs, notes, and other work products that show student understanding.

Reflection: Examine students' work in light of the question, "How did the instruction and supports I provided assist the children in understanding this project?" Although the final product of this lesson will often be examined in terms of how it looks and the quality of the writing, it is also important to consider students' understanding of how advocacy works.

Name: _____ Date: _____

Storyboard

Directions: This template will help you create a story telling the need for some sort of change that will help protect our environment. In the first big box, show the problem facing us, and in the last big box show the end result if the asked-for change is made. In the four big boxes in between, show the steps to get from the first box to the last box. Put captions in the small boxes beneath each box.

Problem:	Step 1:
Step 2:	Step 3:
Step 4:	End Result:

Growing Up Green © Taylor & Francis

Making a Change

*Tracking and Reducing
One's Carbon Footprint*

REDUCING the planet's environmental degradation begins at home. This investigation will help students better understand how their choices and actions affect the environment, and let them consider how small changes in behavior can result in a reduction in their carbon footprint. With younger students, the emphasis will be more upon recording the amount of trash generated and ways of representing this information in a graph or chart; for older students, the importance of estimating how much trash is generated by groups and ways of reducing this amount will instead be the focus.

For this investigation, students will learn how their actions, and those of their family and community, make a contribution to the amount of trash generated each week. Specifically, they will estimate how much waste they generate in a week and then change some of their behaviors to reduce the amount of waste they are personally responsible for. This investigation will help students better understand the consequences of their actions, as well as determine proactive steps they can take to protect the world in which they live.

This investigation can be as realistic as you would like it to be. Students may bring in exemplars of the trash their family generates, which provides them with

DOI: 10.4324/9781003235392-4

a great example of how much waste the class and their families generate in a week's time. This path, although graphic, can also be messy. If you are concerned with the amounts of trash this route may generate, you might instead ask each student to bring to school one type of waste, such as (cleaned and washed) cans used by their family in a week's time. If even this modification might prove problematic, you could also choose to monitor the amount of trash generated within your classroom. There is not one correct way to proceed, but instead a variety of choices. Similarly, the investigation presented here can be completed within a week, but the data collection could easily be extended over a lengthier period or condensed to a single day, depending upon the parameters facing you with regard to time, support, and the mathematical skills of the students involved.

Assessing Prior Learning

Have students estimate their personal ecological footprints, including their carbon footprints, by answering a series of questions. When working with very young students, the questions might be quite simple, such as:

1. How many cans does your family use during the week?
2. How many bags of trash does your family put out for pickup each week?
3. Does your family recycle? If so, how much do you put out each week?

For more advanced students, the questions might be more sophisticated, asking further information such as:

1. Is there material in the waste collection that could be in the recycling bin?
2. How many plastic bottles or aluminum cans are used each week for beverages, such as water or soda?
3. Other than using numbers, can you think of a way to represent the trash you generate each week? If so, show me an example.

Regardless of the questions used, record this information and analyze it for guidance in leading the investigation.

Planning and Teaching

Participants/Grouping: Groups may be small or whole class, and based upon student readiness, interests, or learning profile. If the objective of the learning sequence focuses more heavily upon representing data, using interest- or learning profile-based groups might be the best choice. If instead you want to focus more upon the mathematical operations and estimating, readiness-based grouping might work better, with the tasks assigned each group differentiated by readiness level.

Standards: EfS Standard 2.3; CCSS.MATH.CONTENT.K.MD.B, 1.MDA.A

ACTIVITY 3.1
Power Ninjas

Objective

Students will be introduced to the concept of recycling, the making use of items that have exhausted their original use. Although most students will already be familiar with the idea that recycling involves placing certain items, such as glass bottles, aluminum cans, paper, and the like, in a bin that is taken away periodically, this investigation will help them understand that many items that one would otherwise throw away might be reused in another way than originally intended.

Modifications

Depending upon the ages, skills, and prior experiences of students, the learning sequence may be modified to concentrate upon different skills. If the class or groups of students within the class evidence advanced skills, the focus of the lesson might concentrate more upon estimation and mathematical operations. For students who are younger or who demonstrate lower abilities, representing data might instead be the emphasis of the activities.

Materials

- Student copies of Handout 3.1: Power Ninja Chart
- Teacher's copy of Mary Nhin's *Earth Ninja: A Children's Book About Recycling, Reducing, and Reusing*
- Trash bag
- Clean and empty recyclables, such as plastic water bottles, aluminum cans, cereal boxes, containers from frozen foods, and the like
- Chart paper, whiteboard, SMART Board, or other way to record student responses and display them
- Blank sheets of paper for each student
- Chart paper, construction paper squares (each representing 10 actions), glue sticks, and markers

Instructional Sequence

Introduction and Motivation: Display for the class a trash bag full of (cleaned and emptied) garbage—include items such as plastic water bottles, aluminum cans, cereal boxes, etc. Ask students about what types of garbage they produce at home. Record their answers on a chart or SMART Board.

Procedures:

1. Read Mary Nhin's *Earth Ninja: A Children's Book About Recycling, Reducing, and Reusing* to the class. The book uses a series of ninja characters to help students understand the environment and their role in sustaining or degrading it. One ninja wants children to learn how to take responsibility for the Earth, while another is inconsiderate about how he disposes of his waste. One day, the second ninja goes to the beach with friends and notices a turtle trying to free himself from plastic trash. The first ninja explains how trash endangers animals, and the second ninja vows to mend his ways.

2. Ask the class to think about the three R's mentioned in *Earth Ninja*: recycling, reducing, and reusing. Using a Venn diagram comprised of three circles, ask students to list behaviors that represent each of the three R's, charting these on the Venn diagram. Have students replicate the three-ring Venn diagram on their own, and then ask them to work in table groups to determine which actions identified seem to be the most powerful.

3. Using students' Venn diagrams, as a class, have students create a list of "Power Ninja Behaviors." This list should include three or four actions that they think would make the most difference in reducing waste, such as reusing plastic water bottles, making gift pencil holders out of used cans, or creating a compost pile at home to reduce the amount of food waste taken away by garbage trucks.

4. Then, distribute a template that will let each student record the number of times they engage in the target activities over the course of a certain time period (perhaps a month). Show the class how to record tally marks on the template each time they engage in one of the Power Ninja activities (see Handout 3.1: Power Ninja Chart).

ACTIVITY 3.1, *continued*

5. Have students bring their Power Ninja Charts to class, add up the number of times they engaged in each activity, and find the total number of Power Ninja Behaviors.

6. Have students work as a class to prepare a bar graph of the class totals of the Power Ninja activities. For this, provide chart paper, construction paper squares (each representing 10 actions), glue sticks, and markers. Afterward, ask students to return to their desks and complete a chart in the same way based on their personal data.

Closure: Display students' individual charts around the room, and then let the class engage in a gallery walk where they can review and consider the results of their peers in completing Power Ninja Behaviors.

Assessment: During the group graphing activity, observe how students seem to be understanding the process and contributing to the construction of the chart. When they have completed their individual charts, collect them and review students' ability to understand the process and the accuracy of their results.

Evaluation: Using the group and individual charts to serve as examples of students' learning, consider if the graphs provide an accurate representation of the information contained in the Power Ninja Charts. Pay particular attention to the individual graphs, checking to see if each student was able to grasp the concept.

Reflection: Consider how the guided investigation proceeded, thinking about changes you might make if teaching the sequence again. Might you provide students with greater support and scaffolding, or might they have been able to perform as well with less?

Name: _____ Date: _____

HANDOUT 3.1
Power Ninja Chart

Directions: As a class, we have created a list of "Power Ninja Behaviors" that will help make our world a greener place. Please post this chart at home, and each time you perform a Power Ninja Behavior make an "X" in the box indicating the day that occurred. After the time period in which you are collecting these has ended, total the number of your Power Ninja Behaviors.

Sunday	Monday	Tuesday	Wednesday	Thursday	Friday	Saturday

Total number of Power Ninja Behaviors: _____

ACTIVITY 3.2
Famous Contributions to Math and Science, Part 1

Objective

Students will explore the personal aspects of mathematics and science, considering how individuals have shaped the field. Special emphasis will be placed upon the contributions of women and people of color.

Modifications

Examining the personal attributes and backgrounds of mathematicians and scientists is a task that could be extended almost indefinitely. Depending upon the time you wish to devote to this guided investigation, which as presented focuses on a single individual, Katherine Johnson, the scope could be expanded to examine other Black, Latino, or Asian scientists, mathematicians, or inventors. Some of these, with a book that provides a good introduction to each individual's life, include:

- Sarah Breedlove Walker (*Vision of Beauty: The Story of Sarah Breedlove Walker* by Kathryn Lasky);
- Mae Jemison (*Mae Among the Stars* by Roda Ahmed);
- William Kamkwamba (*The Boy Who Harnessed the Wind: A True Story of Survival Against the Odds*);
- Frederick McKinley Jones, Dr. Percy Lavon Julian, and others (*What Color Is My World?: The Lost History of African-American Inventors* by Kareem Abdul-Jabbar); and
- I. M. Pei (*I. M. Pei: Architect of Time, Place, and Purpose* by Jill Rubulcaba).

Materials

- Teacher's copy of Helaine Becker's *Counting on Katherine: How Katherine Johnson Saved Apollo 13*
- A map or other visual representation of our solar system
- Paint and brushes

- Measuring tapes, yard sticks, or other ways of measuring distance
- Chart paper, whiteboard, SMART Board, or other way to record student responses and display them
- Paper, pencils, calculators, and other materials necessary to perform mathematical calculations

Instructional Sequence

Introduction and Motivation: Read Helaine Becker's *Counting on Katherine: How Katherine Johnson Saved Apollo 13* to the class. This book relays the biography of Katherine Johnson, the famous mathematician about whom the film *Hidden Figures* was based. While reading, emphasize how Katherine expressed a love of numbers from a very early age and how she worked throughout her childhood and young adulthood to learn everything she could about numbers and mathematics.

Procedures:

1. To help students understand the contribution Katherine Johnson made to the space program, have the class map out the distance between the Sun and the planets in our solar system. To assist with this process, explain that the planets in our solar system revolve around the Sun, and that the distance of each planet from the Sun is:
   - Mercury—36 million miles
   - Venus—67.2 million miles
   - Earth—93 million miles
   - Mars—143.6 million miles
   - Jupiter—483.6 million miles
   - Saturn—886.7 million miles
   - Uranus—1,784 million miles
   - Neptune—2,794.4 million miles

2. Find a place to create a scale map of the solar system. Ideally, this would be on a blacktop-covered playground or parking lot, but you may have to go to a park to find sufficient space. If possible, paint the planets on the chosen surface so that there is a permanent representation of the children's work, but markers or chalk of some type would work as well.

3. With students, calculate the distance between the planets if each million miles were represented by an inch. (Note. We realize that

ACTIVITY 3.2, *continued*

not every teacher will have access to an area with 300 feet, so we have provided in brackets the same proportions reduced to one-third. Because seeing the great distance between the outer planets and the Sun is the point of this investigation, we suggest not reducing the distances more than this.) The calculations will result in the following:

- Mercury—3 feet (36 inches) [1 foot/12 inches]
- Venus—5.6 feet (67.2 inches) [1.8 feet/22.4 inches]
- Earth—7.75 feet (93 inches) [2.6 feet/31 inches]
- Mars—12 feet (143.6 inches) [4 feet/47.9 inches]
- Jupiter—40.3 feet (483.6 inches) [13.4 feet/161.2 inches]
- Saturn—74 feet (886.7 inches) [24.6 feet/295.6 inches]
- Uranus—148.7 feet (1,784 inches) [49.5 feet/594.6 inches]
- Neptune—233 feet (2,794.4 inches) [77.6 feet/931.5 inches]

4. Once the distance between the planets is calculated and marked, paint the labeled planets on the surface (again, if possible). Have students walk past each planet, perhaps recording its name and the distance from the Sun on a piece of paper held on a clipboard.

5. Back in the classroom, brainstorm the possible uses knowing the distance between the planets would have had for the Apollo space program. Anticipated responses might include knowing how much fuel to have, bringing enough food and water along, planning how long it would take to get there, and other similar answers.

6. Have students list each of the mathematical functions that were used by the class to determine where to place the planets.

Closure: Conclude the guided investigation by sharing the map of the planets with students and teachers from another class. Have each student create an invitation to the event, in which they will explain to others how having individuals who are good at mathematics, such as Katherine Johnson, helped to enhance our understanding of outer space.

Assessment: Review the invitations students created and determine how well they express an understanding of the contributions of Katherine Johnson and others to the space program. Additionally, when students are spacing out the planets, watch how they measure the distance between them and how accurate they are in doing so.

ACTIVITY 3.2, *continued*

Evaluation: Basic proficiency with mathematics is the norm for most students, but understanding *why* skills in this area are important is elusive. Examine how well the class understands that the contributions of Katherine Johnson and others like her stem from their mathematical abilities.

Reflection: As you look back on the guided investigation, consider how students learning about an individual who made great contributions to the space program shaped their appreciation for the event. Consider how you might more often include the career possibilities that are enhanced by mastery of a subject in your teaching.

ACTIVITY 3.3
Famous Contributions to Math and Science, Part 2

Objective

Students will continue their examination of how individuals make great contributions to the sciences, while also learning about the process of patterns in computer coding and that mistakes in the code will cause computer programs to fail or act in unexpected ways.

Modifications

Students who demonstrate an advanced ability to create patterns might be permitted to create much more advanced "codes" than those of their classmates. For those who struggle with the task, giving them templates with some of the code already completed will assist them in finishing the task.

Materials

- Teacher's copy of Laurie Wallmark's *Grace Hopper: Queen of Computer Code*
- Chart paper, whiteboard, SMART Board, or other way to record student responses and display them as part of a KWL chart
- Student access to computers, tablets, phones, or other electronic devices with Internet access
- LCD projector, SMART Board, or other device that will allow you to show students how to navigate the Hour of Code website
- Cameras or video recording devices for capturing images of students participating in the activity
- Paper and a printer for producing certificates

ACTIVITY 3.3, *continued*

Instructional Sequence

Introduction and Motivation: Read Laurie Wallmark's *Grace Hopper: Queen of Computer Code* to the class. Using a KWL chart, ask students what they Know about computers and what they may have questions about or Want to learn. (Students will revisit what they have Learned at the end of the activity.)

Procedures:

1. Grace Hopper made many contributions to computer science, but none were more significant than her work on coding and the processes of debugging code that has already been written. Hopper created the programming language COBOL, which continues to be used today. To build these skills, you might use the Hour of Code website (https://hourofcode.com/us) to introduce the class to computer coding:

   - Prepare to lead this guided investigation by watching Hour of Code's how-to video (https://hourofcode.com/us/how-to).
   - Plan where you will conduct the Hour of Code—will it be in the classroom or a computer lab? Will students use laptops or tablets? How many students will participate at any one time?
   - Select one or more of the "unplugged" activities to build students' understanding of code.
   - Select one of 20 tutorials that introduce coding through fun puzzles, art, and stories.
   - Try out the tutorial yourself before sharing this with students, as some are more age-appropriate than others.
   - To begin coding, have students visit https://hourofcode.com/us/learn and try out the tutorial you have selected.

2. Share the results of your Hour of Code session with other classrooms, school administrators, and parents. Have the class explain to others what they have done, and share their work publicly. Depending upon available resources, this might occur in a computer lab, an auditorium, or your classroom.

3. Print out certificates and stickers and consider ordering custom t-shirts for the class.

4. Share videos and photographs of the class's experience on the Hour of Code website.

ACTIVITY 3.3, *continued*

5. Encourage students to pursue other online experiences and consider attending a one-hour in-person session to learn more about coding.

Closure: Have your students write a letter to Grace Hopper, telling her of their experiences with the Hour of Code and which, if any, activities they enjoyed the most. Return to the KWL chart and fill out the additional information that students feel they learned as a result of the Hour of Code activity.

Assessment: While students are engaged in the Hour of Code activity, monitor them to ensure that they are on task and understanding the tutorial. Additionally, collect and review the letters the class wrote to Grace Hopper to ascertain their level of understanding of the process.

Evaluation: Think about which students embraced this activity and demonstrated an understanding of the process of coding. Were these the students you expected to excel? Which students have surprised you with how well they did? Why might you have overlooked these students when anticipating who would be successful with this activity? How might you better serve these students in the future? Are there other activities you can include in the future that would continue to permit them to build upon this experience?

Reflection: Think about how the class connected with the process of coding. Did this instructional sequence help them better understand the processes that undergird computer science? How might you incorporate similar experiences into your curriculum in the future?

System Thinking

Green Manufacturing Processes

ALTHOUGH recycling is an important tool in protecting the planet, decisions can be made *before* manufacturing that greatly reduce the consequences of any processes and promote more sustainable behavior. This investigation will consider how changes in the manufacturing process result in using fewer natural resources, reducing pollution and waste, recycling and reusing materials, and moderating emissions.

Obviously, students will not begin manufacturing a product at any date soon. Exposure to the process of green manufacturing, however, especially thinking about how an item might be reused or disposed of after its active life has expired, will help them make better decisions as consumers of merchandise, especially as they look at how their choices have lasting consequences for the world in which they live.

As part of this guided investigation, students will gain a better understanding of the origins of the goods they use and learn about the various factors to think about when making a purchase. These factors include how the Earth is affected by the manufacturing of a product, other uses to which the goods may be put after their original use has ended, and where and how something may be disposed of after its useful life has ended. Students will be exposed to the con-

47 DOI: 10.4324/9781003235392-5

cepts of recycling and landfills, and the problems associated with disposing of certain products.

Assessing Prior Learning

Show the class several items you have in a plastic bag of the type used in kitchen trash containers. The bag might include a box, an empty water bottle, a washed soup can, and the like. Tell students that this is garbage that you generated the past few days at your home, and ask them what you might do with these items. Chart their answers, which might include responses such as, "You can throw it away," "You can put it in recycling," and the like.

Planning and Teaching

Participants/Grouping: For this guided investigation, it would be optimal to have students grouped in pairs. This grouping may be based upon student readiness, interests, or learning profile. A key goal of this investigation will be for as many students as possible to be intimately involved in generating ideas, combining and evaluating ideas, and drawing up an action plan. Pairs will assist with this.

Standards: EfS Standard 1.1; CCSS.MATH.CONTENT.2.G.A

ACTIVITY 4.1
Repurposing Discarded Goods

Objective

Students will understand that items they discard produce waste that must then be disposed of in landfills, but many of these items thrown away might be reused or repurposed to eliminate the need of disposing of them altogether.

Modifications

In a class with many students able to work independently, you might proceed to making prototypes of some of the proposed products. Each pair might produce a prototype, or, if time or resources are limited, the class as a whole might select two or three proposed products from the group and proceed to build prototypes of these.

Materials

- Student copies of Handout 4.1: Final Destination of My Trash
- Teacher's copy of *The Dump Man's Treasures* by Lynn Plourde
- Chart paper, whiteboard, SMART Board, or other way to record student responses and display them
- Paper, pencils, markers, colored pencils, construction paper, glue sticks, scissors, and other materials necessary for students to write and create
- A collection of cans, shoeboxes, and other pieces of waste that might be used to store other objects, both to serve as examples and to be used by those students who might have forgotten to bring one of their own
- Space for display of creations, perhaps with cards that identify the name of the product and its creator

ACTIVITY 4.1, *continued*

Instructional Sequence

Introduction and Motivation: Read aloud *The Dump Man's Treasures* by Lynn Plourde to the class. As you read through the story, emphasize that the Dump Man is finding books that others have decided to discard, and that these books will end up in a landfill if nothing else is done. Ask students about garbage that they generate, both at home and at school, and how they dispose of that trash. Have students complete a template that shows specific items they place in the trash and where they think those items end up (see Handout 4.1: Final Destination of My Trash). After students complete the handout, have them share their responses. Ask them what might occur if they could devise ways to use the garbage they would otherwise send to a landfill in another way.

Procedures:

1. The Dump Man seeks out books that others throw away and seeks new homes for them, even though he cannot read. To help students better understand how to repurpose items, prior to this activity, ask each student to bring in a metal can of the type in which soup, corn, or other canned goods are sold. In the event that you anticipate students may have trouble bringing in such items, feel free to collect cans, shoeboxes, and other such pieces of waste that might be used to store other objects.

2. As a whole class, use Creative Problem Solving strategies to generate ideas for other uses for a can, rather than throwing it away or recycling it. Anticipated responses might include using it as:
    *   a drinking glass,
    *   a vase for flowers,
    *   a water canister in which to rinse paintbrushes,
    *   a holder for pencils and crayons, or
    *   part of a walkie talkie, comprised of two cans with a string linking them.

3. Ask students to look at the list, and to consider, combine, and evaluate the ideas, choosing one or two that each student would like to pursue.

4. Provide construction paper, glue, markers, crayons, and other similar resources, and have students decorate their can in a way that will help make it more attractive. Emphasize to students that their

ACTIVITY 4.1, *continued*

chief goal is to create a prototype of a product that provides a new life for goods that would otherwise be discarded. Although this is their primary aim, if the prototype is attractive, it is more likely to be successful and desired by others.

5. Have students arrange their creations, with labels indicating their use, on desks within the classroom and then allow them to participate in a gallery walk, where they will look at their colleagues' creations.

Closure: Ask students to vote for one of their colleagues' creations, asking them not to vote for their own entry. Tabulate and share the results.

Assessment: As you review each student's work, check and see if their creation could function in the way they intend.

Evaluation: Considering the activity, how confident are you that students understood the principle of reusing objects that might otherwise be discarded? If you feel their understanding is shaky, consider how you might better support them in grasping this concept.

Reflection: Looking back upon this guided investigation, think about how repurposing a can could be shared with others. Might it be possible to create gifts for students' families using their creations? Could there be more extensive use made of the created materials? Are there other items that could be repurposed?

HANDOUT 4.1
Final Destination of My Trash

Directions: In each box under "My Trash," draw a picture of a piece of trash you have discarded. In the box to its right under "Its Final Destination," draw where you think that piece of trash may have ended up (such as a landfill, the ocean, in an empty lot, etc.).

My Trash	Its Final Destination

ACTIVITY 4.2
Reusable Products

Objective

Students will extend their thinking about repurposing manufactured products, allowing them to consider how some items are possible to reuse, while others are not.

Modifications

For students who might need an additional challenge, you might ask them to create a "trade show," where the new prototypes might be offered for sale to potential customers. Students engaging in this activity might prepare a catalogue where the various items are offered for sale, with discounts applied if customers purchased a certain number of the product. Alternatively, students might set up displays of the items, with information detailing each item's use, cost, and potential discounts for bulk purchases.

Materials

- Student copies of Handout 4.2: Venn Diagram
- Student copies of Handout 4.2: Second Uses for Items That Would Otherwise Be Discarded
- Teacher's copy of Lara Bergen's *Don't Throw That Away!*
- A variety of empty and cleaned jars (soaked so the labels can be removed), such as a jam jar, a pickle jar, and the like
- Pencils, paper, and other materials necessary for brainstorming
- Construction paper, glue sticks, glitter, contact paper, stickers, and other items necessary to transform jars

Instructional Sequence

Introduction and Motivation: Building upon the concepts studied in *The Dump Man's Treasures*, the class will examine how it compares with Lara Bergen's *Don't Throw That Away!*, a book that examines other ways to reuse multiple objects, including clothes, boxes, cans, and the like. Read

ACTIVITY 4.2, *continued*

Don't Throw That Away! to the class. As you go through the book, point out some of the ways in which the characters reuse items that might otherwise be thrown away, such as how old clothes were used as costumes for pretend play.

Procedures:

1. Bring three different jars in to show the class—have one be the type that is intended for use as a drinking glass after the jam is gone, one that is a typical commercial jam or jelly jar that is discarded after a single use, and one that is a jar used for any other purpose, such as a pickle jar.

2. Using a Venn diagram, ask students how the jars are the same and how they are different (see Handout 4.2: Venn Diagram). Anticipated student responses for the "same" category might include: "all are made of glass," "all were full of food product," "all are made at a factory," or "all get shipped to stores across the country." For the "different" sections, students may reply, "one is intended to only be used once," or "one can be used once for storing jam/jelly and then reused multiple times as a glass."

3. Focusing on the items in the "different" sections, ask the class why the three jars are different. Let students discuss this with a partner, and then chart their responses. Look for the response "someone made them that way," or "someone designed them that way," interjecting with the reply yourself if not given.

4. Ask each student to design a product that might be used for something else after its initial purpose has been fulfilled (see Handout 4.2: Second Uses for Items That Would Otherwise Be Discarded).

Closure: Have students share their reusable product ideas with their peers. If you like, you might assemble all of the ideas into a class book, or with one or two of the more practical ideas, have students work in teams to produce a prototype of the product that might be shared with others.

Assessment: Review each student's idea, considering if they understand the concept of taking something from everyday use and creating a second use that is practical, realistic, and which would not add too much expense to the product.

Evaluation: Looking at this second activity during which students have considered the reuse of goods that would otherwise be discarded, do you

---

ACTIVITY 4.2, *continued*

---

think they are understanding that products such as cans and jars are the output of humans? Are students beginning to understand that conscious decisions are made that affect whether an item might easily be put to a second use?

Reflection: Looking back upon this guided investigation, consider if there is someplace you could take the class on a walking field trip where students could observe other situations in which a product is designed for one purpose and then put to a second use after its initial use is complete. An example of this might be a play area where the soft surface upon which children play is constructed from recycled tires.

Name: _____ Date: _____

HANDOUT 4.2
Venn Diagram

Directions: Label each part of the Venn diagram to indicate the type of jar it represents. Then fill in items that are unique to each jar in each circle, using the overlapping parts only for those elements that are common to two or more jars.

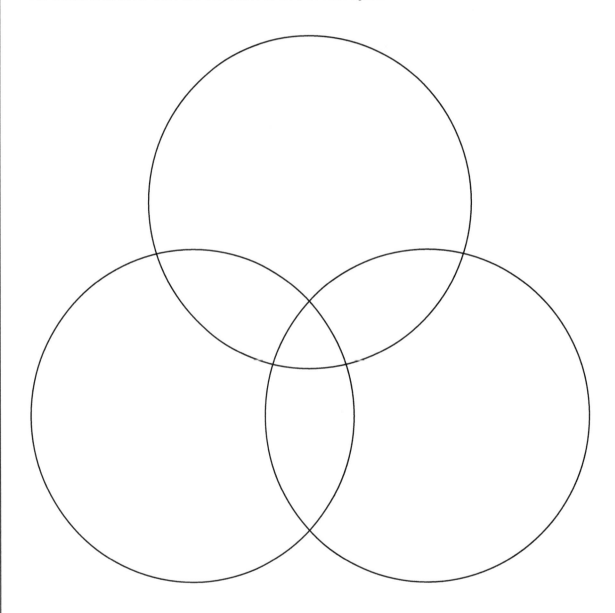

HANDOUT 4.2

Second Uses for Items That Would Otherwise Be Discarded

Directions: In each box under the "First Use" column, draw a picture of something you use every day. In the box to its right, under the "Second Use" column, draw a picture of a second use for the same item, so that it will not need to be discarded.

First Use	Second Use

Investigation 4: System Thinking

ACTIVITY 4.3
Manufacturing and STEM Careers

Objective

Students will build their understanding of the manufacturing process and knowledge of how many STEM subjects are vitally important to those who manufacture goods today.

Materials

- LCD projector, SMART Board, or other device that will allow you to show videos to the class

Procedures

Introduction and Motivation: This guided investigation makes use of a website that allows students to tour and interact with Arconic's Advanced Manufacturing hub in Alcoa, TN. The class will embark on this virtual field trip to learn about how robotics and digital technology have changed the skills needed to succeed in advanced manufacturing, and that being successful in STEM subjects is more important than ever. Decide how best to expose students to this virtual field trip (e.g., a teacher-led activity on a SMART Board, in a computer lab, using tablets, etc.).

Teaching Steps:

1. Introduce the concept of manufacturing by showing the Chapter 1 video available at https://www.manufactureyourfuture.com/Virtual FieldTrip/arconic-tennessee.

2. Have students take notes—do not worry so much about what notes they are taking, so long as they are on task. View the video once more and focus on skills needed to be successful, available careers, skills to be viewed, and types of work done in the field.

3. Talk with students about the terms *intellectual curiosity* and *growth mindset*. Intellectual curiosity is a broad term that involves being curious about what objects are composed of, the underlying mechanisms of systems, the mathematical relationships between differ-

ACTIVITY 4.3, *continued*

ent items, languages, social norms, and history. A growth mindset involves believing that, with effort, each child will get smarter, and that effort, although difficult, ultimately makes them stronger.

4. Next, watch the segment about the electrical engineer (Chapter 2) available at https://www.manufactureyourfuture.com/VirtualField Trip/arconic-tennessee, and ask the class to watch and list the things that she does. Students' lists should include items such as problem solving, programming, debugging, thinking fast on your feet, how the ethernet connects workers in various places, being a member of a team, creativity, critical thinking, and more.

5. Ask each student to write a letter to their adult self, in which they might include a reminder to that adult self of what it will take to be successful in a STEM career.

Closure: Ask students to share their letters with their classmates. They may also take the letters home and read them with their families.

Assessment: As each student reads their letter, observe whether or not they have grasped several of the characteristics and qualities indicated in the videos as being necessary to be successful in a STEM career. Ask each student to indicate what type of STEM career they might like to pursue.

Evaluation: Do students seem to be making the connection between the STEM subjects they study in school and the careers that use such skills? It is important to help young learners make the connection between what they do in school and what careers they might pursue in the future. This is especially true for those learners from lower income backgrounds.

Reflection: As you review the guided investigation, think about how the connections were made between STEM skills and various careers that might be possible for students in the future. Were there places where you might have made the connections more explicit? In the future, is there anyone who works in a STEM field who might come in and speak to the class? How can you better help children make these connections between themselves and STEM careers in the future?

Raising Awareness of the Environment

Global Green Day

GLOBAL Green Day represents an effort for individuals around the world to unite in celebration of sustainability and to advocate for behaviors and policies that support environmentally friendly acts and initiatives. This investigation will look at ways students can connect with their peers all over the globe to advocate for and support a greener planet.

Global Green Day is unique, as it has no set day for celebration. Instead, a group or organization may select a day that is convenient to them and mark that day by recognizing behaviors and actions that are environmentally friendly and sustainable over the long term. Schools of all levels of education are taking steps to reduce their carbon footprint. Low Carbon Day allows all interested primary and secondary schools to participate by having students, parents, and teachers pledge to be more environmentally friendly. On Low Carbon Day, students are taught sustainable topics, such as what constitutes renewable energy (e.g., wind, solar, and hydroelectric power), the impact of climate change on the environment, and the greenhouse effect. On Low Carbon Day, students also positively impact the environment by planting trees, reducing food waste, recycling, riding bikes, turning off unused lights and appliances, and many more activities.

 DOI: 10.4324/9781003235392-6

Communities may also be involved with the green movement through Earth Hour and Earth Day. These events encouraging positive action are popular in the United States, but also involve communities from around the globe. In conjunction with the Peace Corps, Earth Day Network works with local volunteers to implement environmental and civic education programs, tree plantings, village cleanups, and recycling seminars in more rural areas, such as Ukraine, the Philippines, Georgia, Albania, and Paraguay. Earth Day Network also sponsors city and village cleanups, environmental rallies, and educational programs for underprivileged children in India. In Afghanistan, Earth Day Network worked with more than 40 government and village leaders across the country to promote environmental sustainability practices, such as implementing recycling programs and promoting alternative energy.

Reducing the energy consumption of light bulbs and electronics is one of the more impactful steps an individual can take to affect climate change. More than 128 countries participate in what is called Earth Hour, when lights and all electronic devices in homes and businesses are to be shut off for an hour. Earth Hour contributes to the awareness of how much impact humans are having on the Earth through their consumption and is a time to focus on what they have contributed to global warming and climate change. Earth Hour is organized by the World Wildlife Foundation (WWF) and has resulted in lasting change. Global Green Day events provide an ideal way to help make administrators, parents, and teachers more aware of the importance of environmental issues and sustainable behavior, while also providing them with a variety of ways that they can make a positive difference through altering certain behaviors of their own.

Assessing Prior Learning

Send home a survey for students to complete with their families (see Handout 5.1: Family Survey at the end of Activity 5.1). Ask students and their families to complete the survey and then return it to school so that it may be used to determine how familiar the class might be with sustainable practices and behaviors.

Planning and Teaching

Participants/Grouping: For this guided investigation, you might think first about how many booths you plan on having for your Global Green Day. If you plan on having five booths, for example, each should be staffed by two or three students, so this would take 10–15 students in your class. Other key tasks would ask students to act as greeters (2–3) and those in charge of publicity (another 2–3). Students may be grouped by interests or learning profile, although you might also consider grouping quieter children with those who are more verbal.

Standards: EfS Standard 2.4; CCSS.MATH.CONTENT.2.OA.B

ACTIVITY 5.1
Planning for Global Green Day

Objective

Students will begin planning in order to host a Global Green Day that will help raise awareness of environmental issues and sustainable solutions.

Modifications

Thinking of the class's Global Green Day in terms of an event, consider how students will be able to present information to others. You might wish to group students with stronger grasp of content with students who possess the strong interpersonal skills needed to relay the information to others.

Materials

- Student copies of Handout 5.1: Family Survey
- Student copies of Handout 5.1: Members of My Family
- Teacher's copy of *Follow the Moon Home: A Tale of One Idea, Twenty Kids, and a Hundred Sea Turtles* by Philippe Cousteau and Deborah Hopkinson
- Chart paper, whiteboard, SMART Board, or other way to record student responses and display them
- Pencils, crayons, markers, or other writing instruments

Instructional Sequence

Introduction and Motivation: Read to students *Follow the Moon Home* by Philippe Cousteau and Deborah Hopkinson. This book involves a teacher who asks her class to participate in a community action project. Their first charge is to "Find a problem to solve (use your eyes, ask questions)." After reading the book, discuss with the class the importance of raising the consciousness of kids, their families, and the community regarding green issues.

ACTIVITY **5.1**, *continued*

Procedures:

1. Discuss with the class the idea of hosting a Global Green Day for the community to help people better understand environmental challenges facing our society and sustainable solutions that will help address these.

2. Using Creative Problem Solving strategies, identify the problems facing the community. Discuss the problems humans cause the environment. If possible, show students photographs of areas familiar to them around the school, such as overflowing garbage cans, erosion, and graffiti.

3. Use the strategy of "five whys" to better define the environmental problems facing the community. A series of these five questions and potential responses to these questions might include:
   - Why do people allow this to happen? (They are unaware of the harm they are doing.)
   - Why else? (Because they do not understand the cumulative effect of the actions of many.)
   - Why else? (Because there are no simple solutions, such as convenient trashcans.)
   - Why else? (Because we don't reward behaviors that are sustainable and beneficial to the environment.)
   - Why else? (Because people don't know how else to behave and act.)

4. With the class, consider the responses to these questions, and devise a group of four or five concepts that students would most like to emphasize. These categories will each be represented by a booth at the Global Green Day event and may include concepts or themes such as recycling, clean water, clean air, our carbon footprint, and smart packaging.

5. Assign students to be part of one of the booths—recycling, clean water, clean air, our carbon footprint, or smart packaging. Tell them they will need to determine how many flyers each booth will need to have to serve all guests. Provide each student with the template for this (see Handout 5.1: Members of My Family), asking each to count the number of people in their families, subtracting themselves. Then ask each group to add together the total number of brochures their families will need.

ACTIVITY 5.1, *continued*

Closure: Collectively add together the sums from the different booths to come up with a grand total. Discuss with the class how each booth will need to prepare the total number the class came up with, plus some extras, so that every person attending the event may collect the handouts at each table, if so desired.

Assessment: Rotate amongst the groups while students are totaling up the number of people in their families to make sure they understand the task. Collect the group tallies from each booth, and check these to see how well students understand the addition necessary to perform the computations.

Evaluation: Watch and listen to see if the class understands the purpose of the exercise. Operational skills are, of course, vital to success in life, but equally important is understanding why students must acquire the skills necessary to perform those calculations.

Reflection: Thinking back through the guided investigation, consider whether there are more opportunities where you can demonstrate the usefulness of mathematical operations and why, because of this, mastering the underlying skills that make these possible is necessary and indeed very important.

Name: _____ Date: _____

Family Survey

Directions: Take this survey home and complete it with your parents. Please then bring it back to school.

1. How often does your family place items in the recycling bin at your home?
   a. Every day
   b. Once or twice a week
   c. Once or twice a month
   d. Never

2. Do members of your family turn off the lights when they leave an empty room?
   a. All of the time
   b. Most of the time
   c. Once in a while
   d. Never

3. How do the children in your family get to school?
   a. Walk
   b. Ride a bike
   c. Get driven in a car
   d. Bus
   e. Carpool

4. When washing hands at a sink, do you:
   a. Turn the tap off
   b. Leave the tap on, but reduce the rate at which the water runs
   c. Allow the tap to run

5. We eat meat as:
   a. Part of every meal
   b. At most meals
   c. Once or twice a week
   d. Never

As a family, we do the following things to protect the environment: _____

_____

_____

HANDOUT 5.1
Members of My Family

Directions: Think of the members of your family who live nearby and might come to our Global Green Day. Put the number of these family members under the column to the right. If you do not have family members in certain categories who will come, that is fine; we are just trying to get an estimate of how many people will attend our event.

Family Member(s)	Number
Parents	
Grandparents	
Aunts	
Uncles	
Brothers	
Sisters	
Cousins	

Investigation 5: Raising Awareness of the Environment

ACTIVITY 5.2
Global Green Day Brochures

Objective

Students will gather the information needed to prepare the brochures for each booth at the Global Green Day event. These brochures will be shared with family, other classes, and the community, and will touch upon important green issues. They will encapsulate student learning about these important issues.

Materials

- Student copies of Handout 5.2: Information for Our Brochure
- Teacher's copy of Francesca Sanna's *The Journey*
- Chart paper, whiteboard, SMART Board, or other way to record student responses and display them
- An assignment chart that displays the groups you have selected (i.e., recycling, clean air, clean water, carbon footprint, and smart packaging) and which students will work with each group
- Student access to computers, tablets, phones, or other electronic devices with Internet access and word processing software

Instructional Sequence

Introduction and Motivation: Read Francesca Sanna's *The Journey* to the class. *The Journey* is a tale of dislocation, disruption, and displacement, as this child-narrated work relays a family's response to war and violence. After the children's father disappears, their mother plans and executes their escape from their war-torn home. The book personalizes the struggles of many displaced refugees and underscores the importance of being able to advocate for and take action to ensure one's own safety.

Procedures:

1. Refresh students' recollection of the purpose of the Global Green Day event. Ask them to provide the reasons for hosting the Global Green Day and chart their responses. Students' anticipated responses might include:
   - We want to help people understand the problem.
   - We want to share possible solutions with our families.

ACTIVITY 5.2, *continued*

- We want to better understand how to help.
- We want to know more about sustainable activities.
- We want to help heal the Earth.

2. Review students' booth assignments (e.g., recycling, clean air, clean water, carbon footprint, and smart packaging).

3. Show the class several websites that can be used to assemble information for brochures. Older students might perform Internet searches on their own, but the following websites contain excellent information that can be used for this purpose:
   - PlanetPals.com (http://www.planetpals.com) provides activities, guides, games, and other resources that permit children, teachers, and parents to explore green living.
   - Garbology (https://naturebridge.org/garbology) explores the study of what we do with our waste. After we have used items, where do they end up? Garbology uses videos, animations, games, and other resources to help children think about these issues.
   - Discover the Forest (https://discovertheforest.org) encourages children to learn more about forests and provides apps that help them learn more about identifying trees, navigation, geocaching, biology, nature watching, star gazing, and other related topics.
   - Earth Rangers (https://www.earthrangers.com) allows students to download an app that provides access to missions (fun, ever-changing activities that aid in the protection of animals), podcasts, wildlife adoptions, and habitat restoration projects across North and South America.
   - Project Noah (https://www.projectnoah.org) is a global citizen website that supports students' learning about animals and their habitats through missions that permit them to post photographs and other information they have observed in the field.

4. Provide students with a template that permits them to gather information for their brochure (see Handout 5.2: Information for Our Brochure). Encourage groups to include as much information as possible, so that they (or you) may type the information up into a formal brochure later.

ACTIVITY 5.2, *continued*

Closure: Have students begin to prepare their brochures, reviewing with them their calculations from the last guided investigations to determine how many copies will need to be made for their Global Green Day event.

Assessment: While the groups are online looking for the information they are seeking, monitor their efforts to ensure that they understand the assignment, are gathering relevant information, and are on task. Collect the templates they are using to gather data at the end of the day to ensure they are on the right path.

Evaluation: Notice which groups are able to work independently and which might need additional assistance. If a group seems to be floundering, ask yourself whether students are gathering information, but proceeding slowly, or if they seem truly adrift.

Reflection: As you contemplate this guided investigation, consider whether or not this task was too abstract for students or whether they were able to work independently in gathering this information. For those who prove adept at this process, consider whether there are other places in the curriculum where they could be given more freedom and independence. For those who struggle, think about whether a change in grouping or working conditions might better fit their learning profile.

HANDOUT 5.2

Information for Our Brochure

Directions: List information you have found related to each category in the box on the left, and then list the places where you found that information (books or websites) in the box on the right.

Environmental Problem	
Possible Solutions	
Steps I Can Take to Help at School	
Steps I Can Take to Help at Home	

Investigation 5: Raising Awareness of the Environment

ACTIVITY 5.3
Hosting Global Green Day

Objective

Students will understand the difference individuals can make in addressing the environmental issues facing the planet and consider ways to make others consider the global environmental crisis more effectively.

Modifications

With older or high-ability students, you might consider creating an online presence for the event. This could occur via your school's or school district's website or other approved social media. The information contained on these electronic platforms would be similar to that used on posters, flyers, or other paper documents used to publicize the event.

Materials

- Teacher's copy of Melanie Walsh's *10 Things I Can Do to Help My World*
- Paper, pencils, markers, colored pencils, poster board, butcher paper, construction paper, glue sticks, scissors, and other materials necessary for students to write and create
- Letters cut from an Ellison machine, a Cricut machine, or other such letter-cutting tool (optional)
- Copies of brochures students produced for the event
- Nametags (for both students and visitors)
- Invitations for the event, which can be as simple as an 8" by 11" sheet of paper, with space for a drawing on the top half and information about the event at the bottom (i.e., who, what, when, where)

Instructional Sequence

Introduction and Motivation: Read Melanie Walsh's *10 Things I Can Do to Help My World* to the class. Review with the class how important it is to take proactive steps to combat pollution and environmental degradation,

ACTIVITY 5.3, *continued*

and that students' Global Green Day will help to effect the type of change they desire.

Procedures: As you move toward the Global Green Day event, make sure to do the following:

1. Set a date for the event well in advance, such as 4 weeks before the date you anticipate holding the Global Green Day. Send home invitations to the Global Green Day at this time so parents can adjust their schedules. (See Materials list for more information about invitations.)

2. Determine where at the school this event will take place. Most often this will occur in your own classroom, but a corridor, the library, or some other space within the school might work as well. Also consider holding the event with one or more colleagues and their classes—if more students are involved, the event will create a larger "buzz" and provide someone with whom to plan.

3. Decide how you want to decorate for the Global Green Day. The booths might simply be several desks pushed together, but if each has signs and other information posted it will be easier for participants to navigate their way through the event and help students to focus upon the task at hand. More emphasis should be placed on students producing these signs and other information themselves rather than worrying about whether or not these creations are perfect, polished, or professional—this permits students to "own" their event and helps them understand the work necessary to make something happen.

4. Make copies of the brochures that students made, and have students count these and check their count against their earlier calculations regarding how many would be needed for the event.

5. Consider whether or not food or beverages might make the event better. Although some schools have prohibitions about providing food products, doing so can help make attendees feel more special and always proves popular.

6. Practice with students how to run their booths. Review with them a simple formula for doing so, which might include:
   - greeting those who come to the booth,
   - providing a brief one-sentence introduction related to the theme of the booth,

ACTIVITY 5.3, *continued*

- directing visitors to the brochures and inviting them to review the information posted in the booth,
- asking whether the visitors have any questions, and
- thanking them for coming by the booth.

Closure: Hold the Global Green Day event. Permit students to run the booths as much as possible, letting yourself serve mainly as a greeter to the event.

Assessment: Provide visitors to the Global Green Day event with an evaluation form that asks them to evaluate the content and operation of the event. On a more informal basis, observe how groups are doing while working at the booths. Are students interacting with visitors? Are they providing information to them and following the recommended formula for interacting with guests?

Evaluation: Look at the data generated by the evaluations to see if parents and families understood the purpose of the event and what their reactions to the Global Green Day were. Consider how well students seemed to understand the process and if they were able to answer questions directed to them coherently and cogently.

Reflection: As you review the Global Green Day event, consider whether the class's enthusiasm for the subject and event was high or low. If high, you might consider how you could include other similar events within your practice. If low, you might think about how this could be improved should you attempt a similar event in the future.

Everything Old
Is New Again

Initiating a Recycling Program

EVEN the youngest green advocate can help to reduce the effects of our use of goods and materials on the planet. This guided investigation will explore ways that students can initiate and sustain recycling programs, both formal and informal, that minimize the trash headed for landfills from their classrooms, homes, and schools.

Different communities and schools have different recycling options in place. In some areas, no recycling occurs, either at the school or in the community. Many of us live in places where there is some recycling, both at home and at school. And a handful of us live in places where robust recycling programs greatly minimize the amount of trash sent to the landfill, while also helping to reduce the energy expended on the production of glass, paper, metals, and other objects that can easily be recycled. Regardless of the type of community in which you live and teach, this guided investigation will assist students in exploring the many ways recycling can help the Earth.

Recycling programs, of course, reduce the amount of waste that is sent to landfills each year. They also can greatly reduce the energy expended in extracting, refining, processing, and transporting the raw materials and natural resources needed to produce the finished goods that are used by humans before being dis-

 DOI: 10.4324/9781003235392-7

carded. The environmental degradation that often results from mining, harvesting lumber, or other ways of collecting raw materials can also be greatly reduced when robust recycling programs are put into place. Building upon students' growing sense of the consequences that stem from their actions, this guided investigation will help them better understand how concerted efforts on the part of many can have a tremendous positive impact upon our Earth.

Assessing Prior Learning

Remind students of how they have now looked at recycling in several guided investigations. Use a KWL chart to have them list what they already Know about recycling and what they Want to learn about recycling, leaving the "L" column for what they have Learned about recycling until after completing the activity.

Planning and Teaching

Participants/Grouping: There are myriad ways one might group students for this guided investigation. You might choose one option for the entire series of guided investigations, or you might use a different grouping strategy for each. Certain tasks that require multiple products might be conducted as a whole-class activity, while some of the tasks that require stronger computational or communication skills might be grouped by readiness levels. Certain other instructional activities might consider students' interests or learning profiles to place them in learning environments in which they feel they are the most productive.

Standards: EfS Standard 3; CCSS.MATH.CONTENT.2.MD.D

ACTIVITY 6.1
Starting a Recycling Program

Objective

Students will learn about the process of recycling, in that discarded goods are collected and then the materials are used again rather than being sent to a landfill. Students will also gain an understanding of which goods are and are not able to be recycled.

Modifications

In a class with many gifted and talented students, students may group themselves based upon their interest in certain recycling programs, such as aluminum, glass, paper, or plastic. In other settings, consider students' readiness levels, and then provide different groups with different levels of challenge and support.

Materials

- Student copies of Handout 6.1: Walking Field Trip Related to Waste at Our School
- Teacher's copy of Jess French's *What a Waste: Trash, Recycling, and Protecting Our Planet*
- Clipboards, paper, and writing utensils
- Chart paper, whiteboard, SMART Board, or other way to record student responses, draft a letter, create a bar graph, and display them
- Stationary for letter to principal
- Notice to other teachers in the building about commencement of recycling program and schedule for collection
- Plastic bins or cardboard boxes for the collection of recyclable goods
- Signs for each bin or box identifying it as a collection place for recyclable goods
- A wagon, cart, or other device to transport recycled goods that are collected
- Large containers for storage of recyclable materials

ACTIVITY 6.1, *continued*

Instructional Sequence

Introduction and Motivation: Introduce the class to Jess French's *What a Waste: Trash, Recycling, and Protecting Our Planet*. This book is a work of nonfiction, so you probably don't want to take it and "read it through" with the class. Instead, introduce the book, and page through it, making special note of how the work is organized and the different content covered by its various chapters, which include topics such as pollution, household waste, landfill, recycling news, and our future planet. After reviewing the book, discuss the importance of recycling and how it will shape and affect the future of our Earth.

Procedures: A recycling program can be of any scale. It can be a national, statewide, or citywide endeavor. For the purposes of this guided investigation, however, it would be best to create it to operate on a schoolwide basis. If successful, the recycling program can always be extended at a later date.

1. Take the class on a walking field trip around both your classroom and the school itself. If possible, provide each student with a clipboard that has a template for them to take notes. While on this field trip, have students observe and record various types of waste that are being generated and disposed of by people at the school (see Handout 6.1: Walking Field Trip Related to Waste at Our School).

2. When you return to the classroom, record the findings of the field trip on chart paper or on the board so that they can be easily referred to in the future. Record the amounts of various items you find, such as newspaper, paper, plastic bottles, glass bottles, and the like. Multiply each of these amounts by 5, and then discuss with students that this would be the amount of garbage generated each week by the school that might otherwise be recycled. Translate these data into a bar graph, thinking aloud as you do so. Then, have students work individually or with table groups to generate a similar graph to the one you created as a class.

3. Work as a class to compose a letter to the principal asking them for permission to begin a recycling program at the school. While you are waiting for a response, find out where you can dispose of the materials you have collected. In some areas, there are recycling centers where you can exchange materials for money. In others, the

municipality or other local governmental organization will accept materials for recycling.

4. Once permission is granted to begin the recycling program, decide how you will collect materials once a week. It is usually best to provide one recycling bin or container to each classroom in the school, and then to have several in public areas of the school, such as the cafeteria where large amounts of recyclable materials are generated. For classroom containers, simple plastic bins can be used—if only dry recyclables are to be collected, these containers could even be made of cardboard. Public recyclable containers will receive greater use, so consider using a thicker plastic or some other sturdy material.

5. Devise a schedule for when to collect the recycling materials from the other classrooms. The day of the week selected for this does not matter, but it should be one that is convenient for your schedule as well as for other classrooms from which you collect. It is very important that the collection rotation is consistent and that you keep to the same schedule week after week. Nothing will cause other teachers to become dissatisfied with the process more than an inconsistent and unreliable pickup process.

6. At the end of each month, determine how much material has been collected, recycled, and saved from going to a landfill. Prepare a chart for each month, and post these prominently in your classroom.

Closure: At the end of the year, create a master bar graph that shows the total amount of recycling collected and saved from landfills over the course of the year. Display this with the monthly bar graphs, and have students create their own.

Assessment: Over the course of this guided investigation, the class will create as many as eight of the monthly graphs and the final master graphs. Are students learning to do this independently? After you initially model the process, are they able to tell you which step they will complete first and so forth when prompted, and then in subsequent months to describe the steps to you without prompting?

Evaluation: Collect the individual graphs produced by students and check these for accuracy. Are they able to produce their own copies of the graph without looking at the model, or are they essentially copying your work?

ACTIVITY **6.1**, *continued*

Reflection: Over the course of this yearlong guided investigation, students will be exposed to multiple opportunities to display information in bar graph form. Are there other places in your curriculum where they could use this skill? Might this be one way that students select to display information?

HANDOUT 6.1

Walking Field Trip Related to Waste at Our School

Directions: As you walk around the school, what types of waste do you see? Please draw a picture of each type in the box on the left. Then, draw a picture to the right of where you think that trash goes.

Waste	Where It Goes

Investigation 6: Everything Old Is New Again

ACTIVITY 6.2
Understanding Metals

Objective

Students will understand that many metals, glass, paper products, plastics, and the like can be recycled, but that like items must be recycled together, including various types of metal (e.g., aluminum and steel). Students will learn that there are ways to assess metals to determine their nature, including their characteristics, properties, composition, and reactions.

Modifications

If possible, you might conduct some simple chemical reaction tests on metals such as copper, silver, and the like to determine their characteristics, properties, composition, and reactions. Although such work would involve students observing more than participating, if a walking field trip to a local high school, college, or university with a chemistry laboratory is available, it could greatly expand students' understanding of the process of identifying metals. Similarly, advanced learners might investigate other ways of determining the nature of a specific metal.

Materials

- Student copies of Handout 6.2: Is It Magnetic?
- Teacher's copy of Alison Inches's *The Adventures of an Aluminum Can: A Story About Recycling*
- Chart paper, whiteboard, SMART Board, or other way to record student responses and display them
- LCD projector, SMART Board, or other device that will allow you to show videos to the class
- A set of magnets
- A variety of objects, some of which will attract a magnet and some of which will not, such as a wooden spoon, a metal spoon, an aluminum can, a steel can, and the like

Instructional Sequence

Introduction and Motivation: Build upon the experiences students have had with the recycling process by examining the origin and uses of some of the materials they are recycling. To begin, show the class some aluminum cans. Ask where students think the aluminum that make up the cans comes from—Is it grown and harvested? Is it mined? Is it one substance or several? Chart students' responses and refer to these, confirming or correcting them, as you proceed through the investigation.

Procedures:

1. To better appreciate the need to recycle, it helps if students have a better understanding of the origin and uses of the various materials that may be recycled. Read Alison Inches's *The Adventures of an Aluminum Can: A Story About Recycling* to the class. Explore the cycle of aluminum, from its extraction from bauxite rock, to the manufacturing line where it is made into a variety of products, to the store shelf, to a display on a bookshelf, to a garbage can, and finally to a recycling plant. The story is related in a series of diary entries from the aluminum can itself, which is a means of recording data that can be used by students for their investigation of aluminum.

2. Show the Generation Genius video that explores the science of magnets, located at https://www.generationgenius.com/videolessons/magnets-and-static-electricity-video-for-kids.

3. After viewing the video, show a set of magnets and a variety of items, such as a wooden spoon, a metal spoon, an aluminum can, a steel can, and the like. Show how to test each item to determine whether it is magnetic or not. Have students record their findings (see Handout 6.2: Is It Magnetic?).

4. After students have conducted their experiments, have them share their findings with the whole class.

5. Review with students that although many metals can be recycled, they cannot be recycled together. They must be separated before the process can be done. Although two metals, such as steel and aluminum, may appear similar and be used for the same thing (e.g., beverage storage), they have different characteristics and molecular structures.

ACTIVITY 6.2, *continued*

Closure: As individual students share their responses, record these to form a class list of the findings. Display this chart, and perhaps use it as a part of a class book devoted to the subject of recycling.

Assessment: Collect Handout 6.2. Pay particular attention to the accuracy of students' findings, as well as their ability to create a record of those findings that is both accurate and accessible at a later date.

Evaluation: After examining the collected templates for accuracy and readability, consider the following questions: Did students seem to understand the concept? How accurate were their responses? Were they able to record the data in a manner that permits them to use it at a later date? How might the template be used for other similar investigations? Would you need to alter this in any way for that usage?

Reflection: This guided investigation will be relatively brief, of high interest, and fairly straightforward to complete for most students in your class. Consider the importance of accurately recording data and compiling it in such a way that it may easily be accessed and used at a later date to all scientific endeavors. Think about whether your students are being provided with sufficient practice of this vital skill and if there are additional ways you can weave this into your practice so that they become adept at using it.

HANDOUT 6.2
Is It Magnetic?

Directions: Draw a picture of the item examined on the left and write whether it is magnetic on the right.

Item	Is It Magnetic?

Investigation 6: Everything Old Is New Again

ACTIVITY 6.3
Understanding Plastics

Objective

Students will build an understanding of the origins of the plastic bottles and other plastic items that they use every day.

Modifications

For more advanced students, you could ask them to brainstorm ways of eliminating the number of plastic bottles being disposed of in the oceans, in landfills, and along roadsides. You might ask students to work in groups of three or four and generate as many ideas as they can to reduce the number of plastic bottles, with no regard to how practicable the ideas are. Each group could then be charged with selecting one or two ideas that they think most likely to be used and then share these with other groups or the whole class.

Materials

- Student copies of Handout 6.3: Real Food or Garbage?
- Teacher's copy of Alison Inches's *The Adventures of a Plastic Bottle: A Story About Recycling*
- Chart paper, whiteboard, SMART Board, or other way to record student responses and display them
- Student access to tablets or other devices to record videos
- Materials needed for game:
  - Pictures of marine wildlife
  - One rubber band per student
  - A tray or shoebox per every three students
  - Plastic "popcorn" (plastic foam pieces used for packing), ½ cup per every three students
  - Birdseed, dried white beans, or popped popcorn, 1½ cups per every three students
  - A spoon and a cup per student

ACTIVITY 6.3, *continued*

Instructional Sequence

Introduction and Motivation: Continuing to build upon considering the origins of various items that students use every day, this guided investigation examines the origins of plastic bottles. Students will also study ways that they can improve the Earth's environment by reducing their plastic bottle use and recycling or reusing them as often as possible.

Procedures:

1. Read Alison Inches's *The Adventures of a Plastic Bottle: A Story About Recycling* to the class. As a companion work to Inches's *The Adventures of an Aluminum Can*, students will be familiar with the format of the work, which examines the life cycle of a plastic bottle, from its extraction from the Earth, to its processing at a refinery plant, to the manufacturing facility where it is turned into a plastic bottle, to the bottling company where it is filled with product, to the store shelf, to a garbage can, and finally to a recycling plant.

2. To help students better understand how animals can mistake plastic for food, have students play a game. The object of this game is to collect as much food as possible in the time allotted. Because of the short time permitted for collection and the collection method itself, some plastic will be gathered along with the food. (See Materials list for the items needed.)

   - In each tray or shoebox, mix plastic pieces with birdseed, beans, or popcorn. Direct each group of three to "feed" at each tray for 30 seconds, gathering the mix with their "beaks" (the spoons). As each student gathers their share of the mix, they should place the spoonfuls of food into their cup or "stomach."

   - When the 30 seconds have expired, ask students to examine their cups for real food and plastic. Help them count and record the pieces in two columns on the provided template (see Handout 6.3: Real Food or Garbage?).

   - Ask students to return the plastic pieces to their cups and to begin the feeding exercise again. Continue doing this in 30-second increments until the birds' stomachs are full of plastic, at which point they will no longer feel like eating.

   - Ask students to reflect upon the process. What do they think will happen to birds that eat plastic? Anticipated responses might include, "Because plastic is difficult to digest, it can build

ACTIVITY 6.3, *continued*

up in the birds' stomachs and take the place of real food," "The birds will feel full," "The birds will stop eating," and "The birds will slowly starve because they are no longer eating."

3. Clean up the materials, asking each group of students to separate out the plastic and the "food" into two separate piles for collection and storage.

Closure: Using tablets or another recording device, ask each group of students to create a 30-second public interest commercial to address the problems that disposing plastic waste in lakes, rivers, and oceans can cause wildlife.

Assessment: Review the public interest commercials and determine how cogent and compelling students' appeals to the public are.

Evaluation: Consider how urgent students think the situation is and whether or not they have proposed any solutions. Be especially certain to ask: Do students see recycling as a solution to the problem of discarded waste? Are there ways you might extend this understanding to the disposal of other items?

Reflection: This is another guided investigation that will be concluded fairly quickly, but it should assist students in seeing the bigger picture about how pollution endangers ecosystems and wildlife. As with the previous guided investigation, consider the importance of accurately recording data and compiling it in such a way that it may easily be accessed and used at a later date to all scientific endeavors. Think about whether students are being provided with sufficient practice of this vital skill and if there are additional ways you can weave this into your practice so that they become adept at using it.

HANDOUT 6.3

Real Food or Garbage?

Directions: Record the items in your cup that are food on the left and trash on the right.

Real Food	Garbage

Investigation 6: Everything Old Is New Again

Reducing Car Emissions

Using Mathematical Tools to Define Goals and Measure Success

Introduction

Although young children do not drive automobiles, they are often passengers in them. This investigation will examine how students can use mathematical tools to measure how travel by car or other motor vehicles affects the environment, as well as what changes in behavior the children and their families may take to minimize this outcome.

To appreciate the significance and relevance in what is being studied in this guided investigation, students will need to have some knowledge of greenhouse gases and how they affect the environment. Obviously, young children cannot be expected to understand how greenhouse gases interact with the atmosphere to degrade the environment, but even the very youngest child can acknowledge that greenhouse gases exist as the result of human actions and that their presence causes various responses in the Earth's environment. Students should understand that greenhouse gases cause temperatures to rise, which in turn results in other responses, such as the melting of the polar ice caps, rising water levels, and general environmental degradation.

 DOI: 10.4324/9781003235392-8

Do not worry if students' understanding of the effects of greenhouse gases is incomplete. The goal is to help them understand that greenhouse gases are the result of certain human actions, that these cause certain environmental degradation, and that by changing certain behaviors, we can reduce the amount of greenhouse gases produced and the harm that they do to our world. Certainly, if students have had prior experience with the concept of greenhouse gases, you will be able to move further with this guided investigation than if they have not. Regardless, this investigation should help increase their knowledge and understanding of this important issue, and introduce them to some of the mathematical tools that will permit them to track various phenomena and occurrences.

Assessing Prior Learning

Remind students of how they have now looked at recycling in several previous guided investigations. Use a KWL chart to have students list what they already Know about recycling and what they Want to learn about recycling, leaving the "L" column for what they have Learned about recycling after completing the investigation.

Planning and Teaching

Participants/Grouping: For this series of guided investigations, consider grouping students by readiness levels and then creating different tasks at different levels of difficulty for each based upon the readiness level of each group. Students' interests or learning profiles might also be considered for certain other activities, as this would promote flexible grouping.

Standards: EfS Standard 1; CCSS.MATH.CONTENT.2.OA.C

ACTIVITY 7.1
Greenhouse Gases

Objective

Students will learn about greenhouse gases, their history, how they are created, how to measure them, and what steps humans might take to reduce their occurrence.

Modifications

If there are English language learners (ELLs) in the class, you may wish to preteach certain vocabulary so that these students have a foundation in the topic before the investigation begins. Gifted students might also be exposed to multiplication itself, not just grouping to prepare them for it, if this is appropriate based upon assessment data. The understanding here is more significant than mastery of the operations, so use formative assessment techniques throughout to determine if students are recognizing the nuances of the content.

Materials

- Teacher's copy of Anne Rockwell's *Why Are the Ice Caps Melting?: The Dangers of Global Warming*
- Chart paper, whiteboard, SMART Board, or other way to record student responses and display them
- Student access to computers, tablets, phones, or other electronic devices with Internet access
- Paper, pencils, markers, colored pencils, poster board, butcher paper, construction paper, glue sticks, scissors, and other materials necessary for students to write and create

Instructional Sequence

Introduction and Motivation: By this point, you might expect that students will be enthusiastic about engaging in the process of reducing pollution and other threats to the environment. Consider also suggesting that this guided investigation will help their family members to make contributions that reduce greenhouse gases and keep the world safe for them and their future. As you progress through this guided investigation, always be sure to make the connection between mathematical processes and the measuring of greenhouse gases.

Procedures:

1. Introduce the concept of greenhouse gases by reading to the class Anne Rockwell's *Why Are the Ice Caps Melting?: The Dangers of Global Warming*. As you read through the book, explore the various consequences of global warming, such as the shrinking of polar ice caps, the threat this poses to wildlife and humans, and what the future consequences of this may be. Although written in simple language for young children, Rockwell does an excellent job of explaining the greenhouse effect and its causes and consequences.

2. After reading the book with the class, ask students to speak with a partner and to think about what the major causes of greenhouse gases might be. Remind students that many greenhouse gases result from internal combustion engines. After they have had a chance to work with their partners, ask students to share their thoughts. Anticipated responses might include:
    - electricity production,
    - transportation,
    - industry,
    - commercial and residential use (heating), and
    - farming and agriculture.

3. Using tablets, classroom computers, or a computer lab, show students the Greenhouse Gas Reporting Program webpage on the U.S. Environmental Protection Agency (EPA) website (https://www.epa.gov/ghgreporting). This webpage allows one to see and model greenhouse gas reporting data from around the United States.

4. To help make the guided investigation accessible to all students, consider introducing the following terms to the class:
    - emissions,
    - carbon dioxide,
    - fluorinated gas,
    - greenhouse gas,

ACTIVITY 7.1, *continued*

- methane,
- nitrous oxide, and
- parts per million (ppm).

5. Review the major problems with greenhouse gases, including:
   - Greenhouse gases trap heat in the atmosphere, making the Earth warmer. How each gas affects the climate depends on how much of it there is, how long it stays in the atmosphere, and how much heat it traps.
   - Greenhouse gases come from burning fossil fuels for all sorts of everyday activities. These activities include every time we use electricity, heat our homes, and drive cars and other motor vehicles.
   - Greenhouse gases that people are adding to the Earth's atmosphere include carbon dioxide, methane, nitrous oxides, and fluorinated gases.

Closure: Have students work in pairs to create a series of posters showing how greenhouse gases can harm the Earth.

Assessment: As the pairs are working on their posters, observe them to ensure that both students are making contributions to the process. If grouped by readiness levels, this should not be a problem, but if grouped by interests or learning profile, it might.

Evaluation: This is a fairly simple guided investigation, the success of which hinges chiefly on students understanding the concept of greenhouse gases. If this understanding is complete, the guided investigations that follow will be rich and robust. If not, they are essentially math practice with no relevance to students. Having students explain their posters to you is thus a key part of determining the success of the instructional sequence.

Reflection: Think about whether or not students understand that greenhouse gases are mostly the result of human actions and that these gases have an adverse effect on the Earth—one that will be increasingly harmful if permitted to continue unabated. Think about the process. Are there any videos you might find that could show them how greenhouse gases work in an effective manner? How else might you demonstrate how greenhouse gases work?

ACTIVITY 7.2
The FLIGHT Tool

Objective

Students will learn that those responsible for researching, writing, and teaching about the environment use sophisticated tools that help to monitor, measure, and record information related to the world around us, and that a strong grounding in mathematics and data representation is necessary to do this.

Modifications

For more advanced students, you might ask them to devise a list of next steps that they might take as a result of analyzing the information they have gathered on their maps. For example, students might determine there should be fewer greenhouse gas emitters, or that those that exist should be moved so that the list of areas of clean air are more equitable. These ideas could be compiled in a list, and if time permits, each students could choose one to pursue.

Materials

- Student copies of an outline of your state
- LCD projector, SMART Board, or other device that will allow you to show the EPA's website
- Student access to computers, tablets, phones, or other electronic devices with Internet access
- Pencils, colored pencils, markers, and other writing instruments

Instructional Sequence

Introduction and Motivation: Students will use the EPA's Facility Level Information on GreenHouse gases Tool (FLIGHT) tool. Emphasize to the class that this is a tool used by researchers and academics across the world, and that it uses data gathered from many sites and powerful mathematical processes to determine where pollution comes from. Although simplified

ACTIVITY 7.2, *continued*

for young students, this guided investigation will explore cutting-edge technology and ways of tracking pollution.

Procedures:

1. For this activity, you will need an outline of your state. Many of these can be found online. If you have difficulty finding one, use a document camera or overhead projector to project a map of your state and then trace this on paper for later copying. Prepare a copy of this map for each student in your classroom.

2. Visit the FLIGHT tool's webpage (https://ghgdata.epa.gov/ghgp/main.do) and select your state from the pull-down menu. This will generate a map of your state, indicating the total number of large emitters of greenhouse gases, segregated by type, including power plants, petroleum and natural gas systems, refineries, chemicals, minerals, waste, metals, pulp and paper, and other.

3. Click on the map of your state and the locations of the greenhouse gas emitters, divided into segments, will appear. If you click again on the segments, the actual locations of the individual emitters appear.

4. Ask students to label their maps with the locations of the greenhouse gas emitters. You may decide to do the entire state or only the section in which your school is located, or have students work in groups, each one working on a separate section of the state.

Closure: Display the maps around the room. Perhaps invite students from an adjoining class to come and take a gallery walk around the room, looking at the locations of the various greenhouse gas emitters.

Assessment: Examine students' maps, checking to see how accurate they are and if they represent the correct number of greenhouse gas emitters. Listen to students while going around the gallery, checking to see if they are giving accurate explanations to their guests.

Evaluation: This guided investigation exposes students to some of the powerful tools that are used by environmental researchers and policy analysts to track and monitor major greenhouse gas emitters. When you review the maps generated by the children, check to see if they understood that what they were representing were greenhouse gas emitters that affect the environment around us.

ACTIVITY 7.2, *continued*

Reflection: Consider how well students understand that the FLIGHT tool permits them to see in real time the major greenhouse gas emitters in the U.S. as a whole and in their states and communities. Are there other ways that you could check that students understand the use of the FLIGHT tool? Are some students in the class able to use the tool on their own?

ACTIVITY 7.3
Greenhouse Gas Producers

Objective

Students will understand that we are all responsible for greenhouse gas production and that we can take actions that will decrease, or increase, our carbon footprint.

Modifications

With students who might struggle with the concept of mapping skills, you might have them create a map of the school site or its neighboring community where they designate possible pollution sources. To do this you would need to take a walking field trip, have students take notes of what they observe, and review with students ways maps represent a given area of the world.

Materials

- Student copies of Handout 7.3: Keeping the Pledge
- Box set up with mirror attached inside and a cloth/towel over open end of box so that mirror is not seen until towel is lifted
- Chart paper, whiteboard, SMART Board, or other way to record student responses and display them
- Paper, pencils, markers, colored pencils, poster board, butcher paper, construction paper, glue sticks, scissors, and other materials necessary for students to write and create

Instructional Sequence

Introduction and Motivation: Remind students that their previous guided investigation examined identifying and locating major producers of greenhouse gas emissions. Tell students that there is another major producer of greenhouse gas emissions that was not identified using the FLIGHT tool. Ask if they would like to know who that producer of greenhouse emissions is. Assuming an overwhelmingly positive response to that question, direct students one at a time to a box you have set up in another area of the classroom. Caution students not to disclose the major producer of greenhouse gas emissions until everyone has had a chance to see who it is. (Note. On the other side of the room, set a box on its side with a cloth/towel placed over the open end of the box. Inside the box, attach a mirror to the back side so that students will see reflections of themselves when they lift the cloth to look into the box.)

Procedures:

1. Remind students that they, although they do not drive, are one of the major producers of greenhouse gas emissions in the United States. Every time they get into a car for a nonessential trip, they are contributing to the production of greenhouse gas emissions. To remedy this, inform students that the EPA has produced a list of recommended ways to drive less. This list includes:
    - walk or bike when you can;
    - use bike-share programs if your community has them;
    - take public transit when possible;
    - carpool with friends instead of riding alone;
    - use ride-sharing services;
    - plan ahead so that most of your trips can be part of a "trip chain"—if you are planning on being taken to the library, and it is near other places you visit, do it all at once; and
    - play and work at home more often, reducing the need for automobile trips altogether.

2. Ask each student to work with a partner and to consider selecting four of the seven items intended to reduce the amount of driving one's family does.

3. Have each student produce two documents. One will be a poster—have each student fold their paper both horizontally and vertically, producing four equally sized sections. In each section, ask students to draw one of the four behaviors they have selected to reduce driving.

4. On a second sheet of paper, have each student write a pledge. Have students write "I will" at the top of the page followed by their selection of the four behaviors they have selected to reduce the amount of driving they generate.

5. Send home a template with each student so that they can record all of the actions they take that conform with and support the pledge (see Handout 7.3: Keeping the Pledge).

Closure: After a period of 3–4 weeks, have a classroom celebration to commemorate students' accomplishment of helping to reduce greenhouse gas emissions. If desired, post a list of actions they have taken that resulted in reduced numbers of greenhouse gas emissions.

Assessment: Review the poster, pledge, and completed template prepared by each student. Look for consistency throughout these, and determine whether they were able to successfully complete the tally of events that each compiled at home.

Evaluation: The purpose of this guided investigation was twofold: to raise awareness of how our behaviors contribute to greenhouse gas emissions, and to take positive steps to reduce the amount of those emissions. Do you think either or both of these goals were met by this guided investigation? Do students understand that most greenhouse gas emissions are created by our behaviors in our daily lives? Are they making attempts to reduce their activities that contribute to greenhouse gas emissions?

Reflection: Think about other actions kids might take to reduce the production of greenhouse gas emissions. Are any of these practical to pursue in the classroom? Have students changed their behaviors, even in minor ways, to reduce the emissions produced on their behalf? How can you motivate them to continue with these positive behaviors?

Name: _____ Date: _____

Keeping the Pledge

Directions: We have each taken a pledge whereby we promise to take actions that will help protect and preserve our environment. Please post this chart at home, and each time you perform an act that supports your pledge, make an "X" in the box indicating the day that occurred. After the time period in which you are observing this has ended, total the number of such behaviors below.

Sunday	Monday	Tuesday	Wednesday	Thursday	Friday	Saturday

Total number of times I kept the pledge: _____

Growing Up Green © Taylor & Francis

Feast or Famine
Tracking Weather Patterns

A consequence of environmental disruption caused by pollution and climate change is the increase in severe weather patterns. This investigation will look at ways students can track weather patterns in their community and then compare and contrast them with previous years' patterns. Students will look at precipitation, temperatures, and other weather features over the past century.

Weather is already a major part of the curriculum in most classrooms. Students learn to name various types of weather, such as rain, wind, sunny days, snow, sleet, hail, and the like. This guided investigation will reinforce and build upon this knowledge and extend it so that students can also consider weather over time and space.

Reviewing weather patterns for the past 100 years will assist students in better understanding that weather patterns are considered important, that by looking at these we can make determinations about whether or not weather patterns are changing over time, and that such patterns are used to make predictions about the weather we might expect in any given year. Students will also learn that variance in weather patterns is the norm but that recent changes in the average temperature and precipitation are unusual in their severity and divergence.

DOI: 10.4324/9781003235392-9

Assessing Prior Learning

For many teaching young children, you will have a good feeling of their understanding of the various types of weather, such as rain, snow, sunshine, wind, and the like. Many teachers who have also worked on the calendar with their students have a good feel for their understanding of these concepts. If you have *not* engaged in these activities with students, you might engage in a warm-up activity related to weather that will permit you to explore their awareness of weather and calendar. One activity that works well is to have students create a podcast where they record themselves acting as the weatherperson on the local radio station. While doing this, it becomes very apparent which children do and do not understand the weather and calendar.

Planning and Teaching

Modifications: The focus of this guided investigation will be molded by the age and readiness levels of students. For younger learners, or those who struggle with the relatively abstract concepts of time and its passage, the focus may be more upon learning about types of weather than it will be drawing conclusions from data. Conversely, if a class has demonstrated an advanced understanding of the topic, you may elect to spend more time on analyzing the data and making projections from it instead of focusing on weather. If you have students who struggle with the types of weather, consider preteaching sessions where you go over the material you present to the class *before* you do so. Permitting students to become familiar with key vocabulary and concepts before the material is presented increases the likelihood that they will be successful.

Participants/Grouping: For this series of guided investigations, consider grouping students by readiness levels, and then creating different tasks at different levels of difficulty for each based upon the readiness level of each group. Students' interests or learning profiles might also be considered for certain other activities, as this would promote flexible grouping.

Standards: EfS Standard 1, 2, 3; CCSS.ELA-LITERACY.CCRA.W.8, CCRA.SL.1, CCRA.SL.4–SL.6; CCSS.MATH.CONTENT.2.MD.D

ACTIVITY 8.1
Cause and Effect

Objective

Students will investigate and describe human behaviors that contribute to climate change and result in environmental disruptions. Students will also describe cause-and-effect relationships.

Modifications

Students will work with the whole group and with a partner for this investigation. Use think-pair-share or turn-and-talk so that all students can participate in the discussion.

Materials

- Teacher's copy of David Shannon's *The Rain Came Down*
- Chart paper, whiteboard, SMART Board, or other way to record student responses and display them
- Student access to computers, tablets, phones, or other electronic devices with Internet access

Instructional Sequence

Introduction and Motivation: Introduce this investigation by engaging students in a discussion about what they learned in the previous investigation. Ask students to explain why it is important to track weather patterns over time. Ask for a few examples of destructive weather events that were highlighted in the previous investigation.

Procedures:

1. To help students understand the concept of cause and effect and its connection to this investigation, read aloud *The Rain Came Down* by David Shannon.

ACTIVITY 8.1, *continued*

2. Ask developmentally-appropriate questions that illustrate cause-and-effect relationships. Use examples from the book. Questions might include:
   - How does rain affect our lives?
   - What happened to the people in the book because of the rain?
   - Why do you think they felt that way?
   - When someone is crabby, how does their mood affect that of other people?
   - How might we act differently so as not to permit bad weather to make us act differently?

3. Give students a few minutes to think-pair-share or turn and talk to a partner. Allow partners to report to the whole class.

4. Record students' responses on a cause-and-effect chart. We suggest a simple T-chart with two columns, one titled "Cause" and the other titled "Effect."

5. Remind the class about the destructive weather events that resulted in environmental disruption.

6. Introduce the term *climate change*. Ask students to turn and talk to a partner to share what they know about climate change. Explain that many scientists believe that climate change is caused by human behavior.

7. Ask students to think about behaviors that humans have engaged in that might have helped contribute to destructive weather events. They can use the Internet to explore human behaviors or practices that are commonly believed to cause these events. Be sure to use developmentally-appropriate language to help students understand. Examples might include:
   - global warming (effect) caused by too much pollution,
   - landslides (effect) caused by deforestation, and
   - flooding (effect) caused by building homes or businesses in flood zones.

8. Give students time to explore developmentally appropriate websites, apps, or children's books that would help them gather information on causes and effects of these disruptive weather events. The websites, apps, and children's books referenced in the appendices may be used for this.

9. Provide a sheet of chart paper per pair of students, and ask them to pick one human behavior that is the cause for a destructive weather event. This should be drawn on half of the paper. On the other half of the paper, they should draw the effect that they feel is associated. On the bottom of the chart paper, students should write details for the cause-and-effect event that is portrayed on their charts.

10. Allow pairs to share their work with the class.

Closure: Ask students to revisit the learning objectives for the day's lesson. Preview the next investigation by telling them that they will learn ways that they can help make a difference.

Assessment: Assess individual and whole-class learning based on the class discussion and how pairs completed their cause-and-effect chart.

Evaluation: Analyze the effectiveness of this investigation at an individual and small-group/partner level. Determine whether students understood the concept of cause and effect based upon their discussion responses and the completed cause-and-effect chart.

Reflection: If students have grasped the concept of human actions that have contributed to weather-related environmental disruption, you can prepare them for next investigation. If you determine that reteaching is necessary, reflect on what should be done differently and whether the whole class or individual students need reteaching.

ACTIVITY 8.2
Reducing Environmental Disruption

Objective

Students will discuss and develop a plan of action to reduce environmental disruption caused by pollution and climate change. They will each create a project to represent their plan.

Modifications

Students will work independently using a variety of methods. Students may choose more traditional displays of their work, such as a diorama or traditional report or poster, or they may choose alternative methods to display their work, such as creating a video message or podcast. Their selection should be guided by their interest and ability to convey the content to be shared.

Materials

- LCD projector, SMART Board, or other device that will allow you to show videos to the class
- Chart paper, whiteboard, SMART Board, or other way to record student responses and display them

Instructional Sequence

Introduction and Motivation: Introduce the investigation by engaging students in a discussion about what they learned in the two previous investigations. Make sure to discuss weather patterns over time and disruptive weather events and the effect they had on people or populations. Get students excited about the idea that they can do something about it! You might do this by creating excitement and energy through a call-and-response activity or a classroom cheer or a class song that excites the class.

ACTIVITY 8.2, *continued*

Procedures:

1. To help students understand the concept of advocacy, action, and change, remind students of their ages and ask them if children can really do anything to change the way that people in the world think about global warming.
   * If they say no, engage in a discussion about why not. Capture their ideas in writing.
   * If they say yes, engage in a discussion about what they could do. Capture their ideas in writing.

2. Share the video on climate change and youth advocacy titled "Greta Thunberg Is Leading a Global Climate Movement" on the Great Big Story YouTube channel (https://www.youtube.com/watch?v=u RgJ-22S_Rs) or another similar video.

3. Invite students to share their thoughts about Greta Thunberg and her school strike that started a worldwide youth movement. Revisit the original question of whether children can make a change. Remind students that Greta started her movement off small before it became a worldwide movement. Ask students for small ideas that they think they could do that would help change people's thinking and behaviors. Record their ideas.

4. Guide the class through a discussion of what an action plan from a kindergarten or first-grade student should include. Together, agree on three must-have items. Examples may include:
   * what the issue is they are advocating for,
   * why it is important to them, and
   * one small action or behavior they would recommend to begin making a difference.

5. Have students work independently, with support from you, to create their individual action plans. If students want to work together with others who have similar interests, that would also be fine. They may be creative in preparing their action plans, as long as the components that the class agreed upon are present. This allows some flexibility for students to use their individual strengths, talents, and intelligences to demonstrate their learning.

ACTIVITY 8.2, *continued*

Closure: Ask students to describe what they have learned about being able to advocate for reducing environmental disruption. Remind them that young children can make a difference in the world.

Assessment: Assess individual learning by evaluating each student's final product.

Evaluation: Analyze the effectiveness of this investigation at an individual level. Determine whether students understood the concept of creating an action plan of advocacy to effect change.

Reflection: Reflect on the three investigations in this series to determine whether students have grasped the concepts of weather, climate, human behavior on climate change, and youth advocacy. These are particularly abstract concepts for young children, but with developmentally-appropriate instruction and learning activities, they can actively engage and effectively demonstrate their learning.

Systems, Habitats, and Change

How Humans Affect Local Wildlife

DEVELOPMENT, land use decisions, and human behavior have consequences for the birds, animals, and fish that all live around us. This investigation will consider how changes in the students' community that have occurred during their lifetimes have affected wildlife that share these spaces.

This investigative unit will facilitate students' understanding of what habitat destruction and habitat fragmentation are, guide students through an exploration of the local and global effects of habitat destruction and habit fragmentation on the animals that lived in that habitat, and facilitate their engagement in conservation efforts.

For this investigation, students will learn how land conversion contributes to habitat fragmentation and habitat destruction. They will discuss and describe development (new homes, new stores, new roads, new parks, etc.) that they have seen in their communities. They will have a discussion about what had to be removed in order for that development to occur and how those changes might have affected the habitats of animals that lived in those places. Next, students will study animal habitats from around the world, describing the habitats and predicting what could happen if the animals lost their habitat. Finally, students

111

DOI: 10.4324/9781003235392-10

will become Habitat Protection Ambassadors, creating a public awareness campaign focused on local and/or global animal habitat loss.

Assessing Prior Learning

Global habitat loss may be an abstract concept for students. Be certain to make connections throughout the investigation that remind them that habitat loss is global, but it is also local. As much as possible, have students make connections to their current context and then expand their understanding to global contexts.

To assess prior learning, begin by asking students to describe physical changes in their communities that they have noticed over time. Record responses on a classroom chart, taking note of those who do not seem to grasp the concept of physical changes over time. If possible, bring local community photos that show before and after construction. Questions that you might ask include:

1. Can you describe the environment where we live?
2. Have you noticed any changes in our environment, like new roads, buildings, or parks?

Planning and Teaching

Participants/Grouping: For this series of guided investigations, students will work with the whole class, in small groups, and independently, depending on the nature of the investigatory activity.

Standards: EfS Standard 2, 3; CCSS.ELA-LITERACY.CCRA.R.1–R.3, CCRA.R.5, CCRA.W.1–W.2, CCRA.W.5–W.8, CCRA.SL.2, CCRA.SL.6, CCRA.L.1–L.2

ACTIVITY 9.1
Habitat Disruption

Objective

Students will describe local environmental changes and the impact that those might have on animals that live in the area where the changes took place. Students will discuss reasons that changes have been made to the environment, examining pros and cons of different developments.

Modifications

For students who grasp the concept of habitat disruption at the local level, consider assigning them as the "lead investigator" for teams investigating more global habitat disruptions. For students who struggle to grasp the concept of local habitat disruption, provide scaffolding in a smaller group prior to Activity 9.2.

Materials

- Student copies of Handout 9.1: Now/Then Chart
- Chart paper, whiteboard, SMART Board, or other way to record student responses and display them

Instructional Sequence

Introduction and Motivation: Begin this investigation by describing a recent drive you have taken, actual or fictional, where you noticed a lot of changes to the community. You can share with the class that you thought about why this might be happening and that you felt both excited and concerned at the same time.

Procedures:

1. To prepare for this investigation, create a "Now" and "Then" chart, either electronically or using chart paper. Distribute Handout 9.1: Now/Then Chart for students to record responses.

ACTIVITY 9.1, *continued*

2. To help the class understand the concept of habitat disruption, ask students to describe the communities where they live or go to school. Note that some elementary schools are neighborhood schools, meaning that children from the local community attend, and some elementary schools are not, meaning that children come from a range of neighborhoods to attend the school. Thus, the descriptions of the home and school communities may be similar or different. Know in advance which of these two types of attendees comprise your classroom population.

3. Write down the responses on the "Now" side of the chart.

4. Ask students if they can remember any recent changes in the school or home environment. If they are not able to provide adequate responses, be prepared to offer examples, such as a new shopping area, a new park, new homes/apartment complexes, or even a new road. Three examples from the class should be enough to illustrate the changes.

5. Ask students to consider what existed in the space before the new structure. Give them a few minutes to turn and talk with a partner to imagine or remember what was previously there. Provide students with a sticky note to write down or illustrate their responses. Some answers could include trees or grassy areas.

6. Post the responses on the "Then" side of the chart.

7. Introduce the word *habitat* to the class. Dictionary.com defines habitat as "the place where a person or thing is usually found." Help students make the connection to where they are usually found (in their homes).

8. Ask what kinds of animals may have lost their habitat when the grassy places were changed into buildings, roads, or other structures. Make a list.

9. Revisit your initial comments about how you felt excited and concerned at the same time. Engage the class in a conversation about both feelings and record pros and cons. Some responses might include:
    * Why you might have been excited: new places for people to live, new places for people to shop, new roads to help people get around.

- Why you might have been concerned: birds, fish, and animals that used to live in those places may have lost their homes (their habitats).

10. Introduce the phrases *habitat fragmentation* and *habitat destruction* to the class. Deconstruct the phrases by asking students what those words mean to them. Create a word web with their responses. According to The National Wildlife Federation (https://www.nwf.org):
    - Habitat destruction occurs when humans remove trees, fill in wetlands, or otherwise destroy the natural habitat of an animal; and
    - Habitat fragmentation occurs when development by humans breaks apart the natural habitat of animals into smaller chunks.

11. Ask students to consider the impact of animals' homes being destroyed or fragmented. Have students turn and talk with a partner to express their feelings.

Closure: Ask students to consider and describe the impact of local habitat destruction and habitat fragmentation on birds, animals, and/or fish. Allow them to write a short description/paragraph from the point of view of the birds, animals, and/or fish that experienced the disruption.

Assessment: Assess individual learning by reading the descriptions written from the animals' point of view.

Evaluation: Your analysis of students' written perspectives will assist you in determining whether they have grasped the concept.

Reflection: If students have grasped the concept of habitat destruction and habitat fragmentation, prepare them for the next lesson in the investigation series. If you determine that reteaching is necessary, reflect on what should be done differently and whether the whole class or individual students need reteaching.

HANDOUT 9.1
Now/Then Chart

Directions: Use the "Now" column of this chart to record descriptions of the neighborhood in which we live, and use the "Then" column to imagine what this space must have been like before development

Now	Then

Investigation 9: Systems, Habitats, and Change

ACTIVITY 9.2
Habitat Fragmentation

Objective

Students will demonstrate their understanding of habitat fragmentation and habitat destruction by examining habitats from regions around the world. Groups will document the impact of habitat fragmentation and habitat destruction by giving an oral and written presentation to the class.

Modifications

Students can choose their presentation method based on their individual preferences. Students for whom English is not their first language will benefit from being able to work in small groups to discuss and describe different habitats based on photographs from the National Geographic Kids website.

Materials

- Teacher's copy of Helen Orme's *Habitat Destruction: Earth in Danger*
- Chart paper, whiteboard, SMART Board, or other way to record student responses and display them
- Computers, tablets, phones, or other electronic devices with Internet access

Instructional Sequence

Introduction and Motivation: Introduce this investigation by engaging students in a discussion about what they learned in Activity 9.1. Give them an opportunity to share the descriptions/paragraphs they wrote from the perspective of the birds, animals, and/or fish. Tell students that they will be studying habitats from around the world and that they will be learning about habitat fragmentation and habitat destruction.

ACTIVITY 9.2, *continued*

Procedures:

1. To help the class understand the concept of habitat disruption and habitat fragmentation, read aloud *Habitat Destruction: Earth in Danger* by Helen Orme.

2. Use the images from the book to engage the class in a conversation about the impact of the habitat destruction.

3. Explain that there are different types of habitats all around the world that are in danger of being destroyed.

4. Divide students into seven small groups.

5. Allow students to work in small groups to visit the website https://kids.nationalgeographic.com/explore/nature/habitats. They will view photographs and learn facts about seven habitats around the world. These include:
   - grassland,
   - desert,
   - mountain,
   - temperate forest,
   - freshwater,
   - ocean, and
   - rainforest.

6. Ask the groups to decide how to best present the information they learned to the other members of the class.

7. Decide on a list of must-include information items for the presentation.

Closure: Ask students to revisit the learning objectives for the day's lesson. Preview Activity 9.3 by telling them that they will learn ways that they become Habitat Ambassadors, helping raise awareness of the risks that birds, animals, and/or fish that live in these habitats face.

Assessment: Assess small-group learning based on the presentations that the groups give to the class.

Evaluation: Analyze the effectiveness of this investigation at the small-group level. Determine whether students understood the concept of habitat fragmentation and habitat destruction based upon their small group presentations to the class.

ACTIVITY 9.2, *continued*

Reflection: If students have grasped the concept of habitat fragmentation and habitat destruction, prepare them for the final lesson in the investigation series. If you determine that reteaching is necessary, reflect on what should be done differently and whether the whole class or individual students need reteaching.

ACTIVITY 9.3
Habitat Protection Ambassadors

Objective

Students will demonstrate their understanding of the impact of human land use decisions on habitat fragmentation and habitat destruction by creating a public awareness campaign.

Modifications

Students who are particularly gifted in visual arts, dance, music, and/or technology may be well suited to serve as classroom experts in the development of the public service campaign. Additionally, students who speak a second language may be able to contribute language, either written or verbal, that provides access to the public awareness campaign in a different language.

Materials

- An assortment of posters and other student work from prior investigations
- Chart paper, whiteboard, SMART Board, or other way to record student responses and display them

Instructional Sequence

Introduction and Motivation: Introduce this investigation by engaging students in a discussion about what they learned in the previous activities. Tell them that today they will become Habitat Protection Ambassadors!

Procedures:

1. To help students demonstrate their overall understanding that human land use decisions have an impact on habitat disruption and habitat fragmentation, review the posters, definitions, etc., from the previous activities.

ACTIVITY 9.3, *continued*

2. Engage students in a discussion of what an ambassador does. If the school has student ambassadors, use that to begin the conversation. If not, provide the scaffolding necessary for students to understand what an ambassador does.

3. Connect the job description of an ambassador to what it might mean to be a Habitat Protection Ambassador.

4. Write down responses.

5. Ask students to list some creative ways that a Habitat Protection Ambassador could prepare and share their message. Make a list.

6. Give students time to work independently, with support from you and their classroom expert peers, in order to prepare a public advocacy campaign.

Closure: Revisit the learning objectives for the three investigations. Allow students to express their feelings about what they have learned and how they can use that new learning to influence others.

Assessment: Assess individual learning based on the Habitat Protection Ambassador campaigns. Criteria should include the requirements agreed to by students, along with any specifications that you might have for spelling, grammar, etc.

Evaluation: Analyze the effectiveness of this investigation at the individual level, examining students' growth in understanding over the three investigations. Consider inviting families in for an Advocacy Showcase, or some similar family event.

Reflection: Consider the ways in which students took a different perspective, reflected on the importance of maintaining a healthy environment, and prepared a public advocacy campaign. If you had to teach this investigation again, how would you enhance it? Celebrate each student's unique contribution to protecting the environment and habitats of birds, animals, and fish.

Reflection: Reflect on the three activities in this investigation. What changes might you have made to the investigations for students who needed more or less support?

Mapping Better Health

Creating an Outdoor Exercise Park

ONE way to take control over and improve one's health is to make changes in diet and exercise patterns that have a demonstrated positive effect on one's overall well-being. This investigation will be different than the others in the book insofar as the investigation will be geared toward using readily available resources and educating the community; thus, the investigation is not exploratory as much as it is a gathering of resources and ideas for young children. We will discover ways to support the National Education for Sustainability K–12 Standards and the Common Core State Standards with young learners by:

1. examining ways in which students can use available community resources to engage in fitness opportunities,
2. examining virtual fitness opportunities to use with students for whom utilizing outdoor space is not an option, and
3. encouraging students to educate their families and community on the importance of overall well-being and how all members of the community will benefit.

 DOI: 10.4324/9781003235392-11

Growing Up GREEN

Assessing Prior Learning

Have a simple conversation with students to ask them about the importance of well-being and fitness. Ask them about some of the things they do for fitness outside of school.

Planning and Teaching

Participants/Grouping: Students will work in small groups or with the whole class during the various activities in this investigation.

Standards: EfS Standard 2, 3; CCSS.ELA-Literacy.CCRA.W.1–W.3, CCRA.W.8, CCRA.SL.4–SL.6

ACTIVITY 10.1
Fitness Opportunities

Objective

Students will discuss ways in which they can use readily available community resources to engage in fitness opportunities. Students will describe opportunities in each season of the year that would lend themselves to engagement in fitness opportunities.

Modifications

These activities do not require students to write a lot of text. Consider ways in which you would allow young children to express themselves verbally and using images. If you have nonverbal students in your classroom, consider other ways in which they might be able to express themselves.

Materials

- Chart paper, whiteboard, SMART Board, or other way to record student responses and display them
- I Do-We Do-You Do chart will be used with the class
- Construction paper and other art materials, such as colored pencils, markers, crayons, etc.

Instructional Sequence

Introduction and Motivation: Engage students in a discussion about the kinds of activities they engage in when they attend PE class. Ask them to name some of the things they enjoy the most. Share some of your favorite wellness practices with them. For the investigation, engage students by using the I Do-We Do-You Do practice. The chart paper or whiteboard should be divided into three sections: I Do, We Do, and You Do. This is a teaching strategy that will help you provide scaffolding and gradual release for students. You provide students with an example of a concept (I Do), work with students to create class examples of the same concept (We Do), and then allow students to create their own concepts working independently (You Do).

ACTIVITY 10.1, *continued*

Procedures:

1. Tell students that they will be focusing on exploring opportunities outside of school where they can engage in fitness and well-being activities throughout the year. Ask them to focus on each season during the year. Explain that they want to find practices that will help them focus on fitness while also being "school smart," meaning that they could practice a skill that they have already learned in school.

2. Ask students to remind you about the four seasons of the year: winter, spring, summer, and fall.

3. **I Do:** Using your I Do-We Do-You Do chart, identify some practices that you like to do in your community that focus on well-being and fitness. Give one example for each season. Include images and short phrases. Examples might include:
   - Winter activity: skiing (image: snow-capped mountain)
   - Spring activity: gardening (image: garden area before and after flowers or vegetables have been planted)
   - Summer activity: swimming (image: pool or beach)
   - Fall activity: hiking (image: woodsy area or walking path)

4. **We Do:** Divide students into small groups. Give each group construction paper and other art materials.

5. Ask students to think about places in and around the school learning community (other than PE) that they could use to focus on well-being and fitness. Have students discuss.

6. Ask students to think about the communities in which they live. Tell them that they will complete their own well-being and fitness chart next.

7. **You Do:** Have students complete their own well-being and fitness chart, filling in one box per season, including one each for spring, summer, fall, and winter.

Closure: Give students an opportunity to share their work with the class.

Assessment: Assess students' understanding of the concept of using readily available resources by reviewing their posters for the required information.

ACTIVITY 10.1, *continued*

Evaluation: Reflect on this investigation by encouraging students to practice one of the ideas at home and then to come in to class the next day to share what they did and how they enjoyed it.

Reflection: This concept should be fairly easy for the class to understand. If, for some reason, students do not grasp the concept, work with them in a small group to reinforce the concept and to give them a chance to find opportunities in the school environment that would spark ideas that might spill over to the home environment.

ACTIVITY 10.2
Virtual Fitness

Objective

Students will explore and recommend virtual fitness opportunities that can be used when utilizing outdoor space is not an option.

Materials

- Teacher's copies of children's books about fitness and well-being
- Computers, tablets, phones, or other electronic devices with Internet access
- Kids' fitness websites such as:
  - "Fitness" by HealthyChildren.org: https://www.healthychildren.org/English/healthy-living/fitness/Pages/default.aspx
  - Action for Healthy Kids: https://www.actionforhealthykids.org
  - Cosmic Kids: https://www.cosmickids.com
  - Habitz: https://habitz.com

Instructional Sequence

Introduction and Motivation: Ask students to discuss some of the fitness activities from Activity 10.1 that they tried at home.

Procedures:

1. To help the class understand the concept of virtual fitness and well-being, read aloud a children's book about fitness and well-being. Two options include *Shake a Leg! (Sesame Street Series)* by Constance Allen and Maggie Swanson, and *Get Up and Go!* by Nancy Carlson.

2. Engage students in a conversation about reasons that a child their age might not be able to go outdoors. Reasons might include:
   - weather (too hot, too cold, etc.),
   - safety (not safe for children to go outside to engage in fitness activities), and
   - availability (no place for children to go outside to engage in fitness activities).

ACTIVITY 10.2, *continued*

3. Ask students to brainstorm some ways that children who cannot get outdoors can still engage in fitness and well-being activities. Guide students toward virtual options, like apps or websites.

4. Divide students into small groups to investigate apps or websites that would be helpful to a child who cannot go outdoors. Develop a list of guidelines to focus their investigations. Things that they might want to consider include:
    *   cost (low or free),
    *   parental access (can parents check in on me?),
    *   security (will my friends and I be safe if we use this app/website?), and
    *   fun (will my friends and I enjoy using this app/website?).

5. Give students about 20 minutes to find at least one app or website to recommend. Remind them that they need to be able to explain why they picked this app or website.

6. Compile a class recommendation list.

Closure: Ask students to discuss how they would feel about using apps or websites instead of going outdoors. Help them draw the conclusion that such an experience could be fun and beneficial if outdoor activity is not available.

Assessment: Evaluate students' participation in the small-group app/website discovery activity by monitoring the small groups and taking anecdotal notes on their participation.

Evaluation: Use the lists and students' justification for including a particular app/website to determine whether they understood why alternative/virtual options for fitness and well-being might be beneficial.

Reflection: Consider whether students understood reasons why they might need to access alternate/virtual options for fitness and well-being. How might you sharpen that message if you have a classroom full of students who all have access to physical spaces outside of the school environment?

ACTIVITY 10.3
Promoting Well-Being

Objective

Students will educate their families and community on the importance of overall well-being and how all members of the community can benefit from engaging in opportunities that support fitness and well-being by creating a short video clip/commercial to share with families.

Modifications

Students who may struggle with early writing skills but who have the ability to use technology to communicate with others may be well suited to organize the other students in the small group during the video activity.

Materials

- Chart paper, whiteboard, SMART Board, or other way to record student responses and display them
- A film director's reel and some props connected to being a filmmaker
- Several exemplars from previous investigations
- Student access to tablets or other devices to record videos
- Construction paper, poster board, butcher paper, stickers, scissors, glue sticks, etc.

Instructional Sequence

Introduction and Motivation: Find a film director's reel and some props connected to being a filmmaker. Wear/carry those at the beginning of this investigation and tell students that they will be making their very own fitness and well-being commercials to share with their families.

Procedures:

1. Begin by reviewing what you covered in the previous activities.
2. Ask students to remind you about the list of activities that can be completed in winter, spring, summer, and fall.

ACTIVITY 10.3, *continued*

3. Ask students to remind you about reasons why a child their age might not be able to go outdoors to participate in fitness and well-being activities. Discuss the virtual options that the class developed.

4. Ask students for ideas about how they can share their learning with families using video. Engage them in a discussion about what items would be important to effectively communicating a message. Items may include:
    * visual props,
    * predetermined language/script,
    * appropriate music, and
    * appropriate demonstration of a fitness or well-being activity to illustrate the importance of the cause.

5. Divide students into "film crews." Ask them to draft ideas for their commercials. This should be done with your support and that of a classroom assistant and/or parent volunteer.

6. Give students an opportunity to practice, review, refilm, and finalize their commercials.

7. Share the commercials with the class.

Closure: Tell students that you will be sharing the videos/commercials that they made with families via whatever classroom communication tool you currently use. Ask them to help you spread the word to their families by sharing the goals of the assignment and previewing a little of their work when the family is together in the evening.

Assessment: Assess students' ability to articulate the importance of engaging in fitness and well-being activities to their families by reviewing their short video clips to confirm that they have shared relevant and important details.

Evaluation: Analyze the effectiveness of this series of investigations by reviewing all of the work samples that were submitted by students. Pay particular attention to their language growth and advocacy related to using available, low-cost resources.

Reflection: Reflect on the lessons in this investigation. Although loosely connected, the idea was to get children to become more aware of the importance of fitness and well-being, options related to accessing fitness and well-being activities, and to help them spread the message to their

ACTIVITY **10.3**, *continued*

families about why fitness and well-being are important. If your students completed this series better able to understand and articulate the things described previously, how could you enhance that if you had longer to teach this investigation?

References

Adler, M. J. (Ed.). (1984). *The Paideia program: An educational syllabus*. The Institute for Philosophical Research.

Brisk, M. E., & Harrington, M. M. (2007). *Literacy and bilingualism: A handbook for ALL teachers* (2nd ed.). Erlbaum.

Bruner, J. S. (1966). *Toward a theory of instruction*. The Belknap Press of Harvard University Press.

Cunningham, W. P., & Saigo, B. W. (2001). *Environmental science: A global concern* (6th ed.). McGraw-Hill.

Helm, J. H., & Katz, L. (2011). *Young investigators: The project approach in the early years* (2nd ed.). Teachers College Press.

Isaksen, S. G., Dorval, K. B., & Treffinger, D. J. (2011). *Creative approaches to problem solving: A framework for innovation and change* (3rd ed.). SAGE.

Johnson, S. K., & Kendrick, J. (Eds.). (2005). *Science education for gifted learners*. Prufrock Press.

Perkins, D. (1992). *Smart schools: Better thinking and learning for every child*. The Free Press.

Renzulli, J. S., & Reis, S. M. (2014). *The Schoolwide Enrichment Model: A how-to guide for talent development* (3rd ed.). Prufrock Press.

Schroth, S. T. (2007). Gifted English language learners: Developing talent while supporting English language acquisition. *Gifted Education Press Quarterly, 21*(2), 5–9.

Schroth, S. T. (2018). Saving the planet, stretching their skills: Using environmental science investigations to challenge gifted children. *Parenting for High Potential, 7*(1), 4–8.

Schroth, S. T., Daniels, J., & McCormick, K. (2019). Altered carbon: How parents can encourage and support gifted children's interest in STEM with readily available tools and apps. *Parenting for High Potential, 8*(1), 15–18.

Schroth, S. T., & Helfer, J. A. (2018). *Developing teacher diversity in early childhood and elementary education: The REACH program approach.* Palgrave Macmillan.

Schroth, S. T., Helfer, J. A., Beck, D. L., & Swanson, B. L. (2011). *Planning differentiated instruction & assessing results: Teaching to assure each student's success.* Kendall Hunt.

Schroth, S. T., Helfer, J. A., LaRosa, D. M., Lanfair, J. K., & Mahone, C. D. (2011). Integrating sustainability education concepts into K–12 curriculum. In J. Newman (Ed.), *Green education: An A-to-Z guide.* SAGE.

Smutny, J. F. (2016). *Teaching gifted children in today's preschool and primary classrooms: Identifying, nurturing, and challenging children ages 4–9.* Free Spirit.

Smutny, J. F., & von Fremd, S. E. (2010). *Differentiating for the young child: Teaching strategies across the content areas, PreK–3* (2nd ed.). Corwin.

Spellman, F. R., & Stoudt, M. (2013). *Environmental science: Principles and practices.* Scarecrow Press.

Tomlinson, C. A. (2003). *Fulfilling the promise of the differentiated classroom: Strategies and tools for responsive learning.* Association for Supervision and Curriculum Development.

Tomlinson, C. A. (2014). *The differentiated classroom: Responding to the needs of all learners* (2nd ed.). Association for Supervision and Curriculum Development.

Tomlinson, C. A., Kaplan, S. N., Renzulli, J. S., Purcell, J. H., Leppien, J. H., Burns, D. E., Strickland, C. A., & Imbeau, M. B. (2009). *The parallel curriculum: A design to develop learner potential and challenge advanced learners* (2nd ed.). Corwin.

Treffinger, D. J., Isaksen, S., & Stead-Doval, B. (2006). *Creative problem solving: An introduction* (4th ed.). Prufrock Press.

Treffinger, D. J., Young, G. C., Nassab, C. A., & Wittig, C. V. (2004). *Enhancing and expanding gifted programs: The levels of service approach.* Prufrock Press.

Appendix A
Children's Literature About Sustainability

Title	Author(s)	Sustainability Themes
10 Things I Can Do to Help My World	Melanie Walsh	Colorful and attractive nonfiction book that sets forth 10 simple and practical ways children can address environmental degradation through sustainable behaviors.
A Different Pond	Bao Phi	A Caldecott Honor book that relays the story of a young boy who goes fishing at dawn at a lake outside of Minneapolis, where his father tells him of a similar lake in his native Vietnam.
Counting on Katherine: How Katherine Johnson Saved Apollo 13	Helaine Becker	Relays the life history of Katherine Johnson, whose early skills in mathematics ultimately led to her working for NASA to assist the Apollo space program.
Don't Throw That Away!: A Lift-the-Flap Book About Recycling and Reusing	Lara Bergen	Following the escapades of an environmental superhero, the book explores the ways common household items can be recycled and reused.

Title	Author(s)	Sustainability Themes
Earth Ninja: A Children's Book About Recycling, Reducing, and Reusing	Mary Nhin	Charming and clever story about a small ninja who shows his friends how to protect the Earth by recycling, reducing waste, and reusing items.
Follow the Moon Home: A Tale of One Idea, Twenty Kids, and a Hundred Sea Turtles	Philippe Cousteau and Deborah Hopkinson	Beautifully illustrated tale by a well-known environmental activist that shows how even the youngest children can make a powerful difference in their world.
Get Up and Go!	Nancy Carlson	Encourages young children to participate in movement and exercise and explores the benefits of going outside to engage in fitness.
Grace Hopper: Queen of Computer Code	Laurie Wallmark	Biography of Grace Hopper, a pioneer in the field of computer coding, focusing upon some of her greatest challenges and accomplishments.
Habitat Destruction: Earth in Danger	Helen Orme	Explores how animals around the world are losing their habitats due to industrial development and environmental changes, causing many of them to become endangered.
Maybe Something Beautiful: How Art Transformed a Neighborhood	F. Isabel Campoy and Theresa Howell	Tells the true story of how a young girl living in San Diego transformed her neighborhood through a series of community murals.
Mae Among the Stars	Roda Ahmed	An examination of the life of Mae Jemison, the first Black female astronaut, with an emphasis on her education and preparation for this occupation.
One Plastic Bag: Isatou Ceesay and the Recycling Women of the Gambia	Miranda Paul	Tells the story of a Gambian woman who addressed the problem plastic bags were causing the environment while also creating an indigenous industry.

Title	Author(s)	Sustainability Themes
Rachel Carson and Her Book That Changed the World	Laurie Lawlor	A biography of eminent environmentalist, Rachel Carson, whose book *Silent Spring* is credited by some as beginning the modern environmental movement.
Redwoods	Jason Chin	A boy riding on a subway finds a book about redwoods, and while reading it, is transported to California to learn more about the trees.
Shake a Leg! (Sesame Street)	Constance Allen and Maggie Swanson	Encourages young children to participate in movement and exercise using language that is friendly to very young children.
The Adventures of a Plastic Bottle: A Story About Recycling	Alison Inches	Tells the journey of a plastic bottle, from the refinery, to the manufacturing line, to the store shelf, to a recycling bin, to its new life as a fleece jacket.
The Adventures of an Aluminum Can: A Story About Recycling	Alison Inches	Told through the diary entries of an aluminum can, this book shows its life cycle, from its beginnings as ore within bauxite rock, then through a manufacturing line, its sale in a store, its use at home, and finally, its trip to a recycling plant.
The Boy Who Harnessed the Wind: A True Story of Survival Against the Odds	William Kamkwamba	A boy who lives in a tiny village in Malawi builds a windmill out of old bicycle parts and scrap metal, providing his family with electricity and water necessary to survive and prosper despite a drought.
The Dump Man's Treasures	Lynn Plourde	Mr. Pottle, who runs the town dump, cannot read. Despite this, he works to find homes for discarded books, helping to teach his neighbors the value of both reading and reusing/recycling.
The Journey	Francesca Sanna	Beautifully illustrated tale of a family whose lives are disrupted by war and death, forcing them to leave their home for a new life in a new country.

Title	Author(s)	Sustainability Themes
The Rain Came Down	David Shannon	A neighborhood where disagreeable, argumentative neighbors undergo a change in attitude and behavior as the result of the rain stopping, the sun coming out, and a rainbow appearing.
The Tree Lady: The True Story of How One Tree-Loving Woman Changed a City Forever	H. Joseph Hopkins	The story about a young teacher who had grown up amongst the redwoods of northern California who moved to San Diego, where there were almost no trees, and what she did to remedy that.
The Water Princess	Susan Verde	True story of an African girl who works to improve her community's access to potable water with which they can drink, cook, and clean.
What Color Is My World?: The Lost History of African-American Inventors	Kareem Abdul-Jabbar	Profiles of a variety of African American inventors who used ingenuity, hard work, and perseverance to make our world safer, better, and brighter.
What a Waste: Trash, Recycling, and Protecting Our Planet	Jess French	A heavily illustrated nonfiction work that explores the problems of waste and pollution and relays the shocking facts about where our waste goes.
Why Are the Ice Caps Melting? The Dangers of Global Warming	Anne Rockwell	Friendly and accessible book explores why the climate is changing, what dangers this causes, and some steps we may take to address this.
Wolf in the Snow	Matthew Cordell	A young child and a wolf cub are both lost in the snow in this 2018 Caldecott Medal-winning book, which relays the tale of how friendship and trust developed between two friends from very different backgrounds.

Appendix B
Useful Websites and Apps

Title	URL	Description
Action for Healthy Kids	https://www.actionfor healthykids.org	National nonprofit dedicated to creating healthy school environments for children.
Climate Kids	https://climate kids.nasa.gov/ weather-climate	NASA website geared toward children to teach them about weather and climate change.
Cosmic Kids	https://www.cosmickids.com	Yoga and wellness activities directed to help children embrace mindfulness and wellness.
Cosmic Kids (App)	App Store or Google Play	Free app that contains yoga and mindfulness activities for children ages 3 to 9.
Dictionary.com	https://www.dictionary.com	Online dictionary with definitions, synonyms, antonyms, and other features.
Discover the Forest	https://discover theforest.org	A collection of activities that permit children and their families to study nature, identify trees, track wildlife, and a variety of other topics.

Title	URL	Description
Earth Rangers	https://www.earthrangers.com	A free app that permits children to build backyard habitats, protect marine animals from pollution, and make forest-friendly crafts.
FLIGHT	https://ghgdata.epa.gov/ghgp/main.do	Facility Level Information on GreenHouse gases Tool (FLIGHT) that shows the location of greenhouse gas emitters.
Garbology	https://naturebridge.org/garbology	A subsection of the NatureBridge website that explores the study of what happens to our garbage and where it ends up.
Generation Genius	https://www.generationgenius.com/videolessons/magnets-and-static-electricity-video-for-kids	A series of videos and other online instructional experiences and materials that explore STEM subjects.
Great Big Story	https://www.youtube.com/channel/UCajXeitgFL-rb5-gXI-aG8Q/featured	A YouTube channel devoted to short documentaries and films covering a number of themes, including the environment.
Green Map System	http://www.greenmap.org/greenhouse/about	Provides tools for mapmaking that permit children to create maps that show the cultural and environmental state of their communities.
Habitz	App Store or Google Play	Free app that that has parental controls and allows children as young as 4 years old to track their fitness goals.
Healthy Children	https://www.healthychildren.org/English/healthy-living/fitness/Pages/default.aspx	Hosted by pediatricians, it encourages ways to engage with children around fitness and well-being.

Title	URL	Description
Hour of Code	https://hourofcode.com/us	A one-hour introduction to computer science, designed to explain the coding process, let anyone learn the basics of coding, and increase participation of girls and diverse learners.
Manufacture Your Future	https://www.manufactureyourfuture.com	Materials, virtual tours, and curricular materials rooted in STEM principles to help cultivate the next generation of manufacturing innovators and leaders.
National Geographic Kids	https://kids.nationalgeographic.com	America's largest geographical organization, devoted to preserving wildlife and the environment for more than 130 years, provides a variety of educational resources, including films, reports, and games.
PlanetPals	http://www.planetpals.com	A collection of games, videos, and other materials designed to help children learn more about the environment, endangered species, and other related issues and themes.
Project Noah	https://www.projectnoah.org	A platform that permits children from around the world to identify, share, and discover wildlife.
The National Wildlife Federation	https://www.nwf.org	One of the largest and most influential conservation organizations, the site provides a variety of wildlife and nature guides as well as other educational resources.
U.S. Environmental Protection Agency	https://www.epa.gov/ghgreporting	Greenhouse gas reporting tool at the U.S. EPA website that permits modeling of various greenhouse gas emitters.

Appendix C
Standards for Sustainability Education

Many states, school districts, and schools try to adhere to student learning standards for all teaching and learning that occurs within their jurisdiction, schools, or classrooms. This effort stems from the standards-based education movement, which calls for clear, measurable standards for what students should know, understand, and be able to do as a result of a sequence of instruction. Standards-based instruction is preferable to norm-referenced rankings, because rather than comparing students' learning to that of their peers, it instead provides a concrete standard that student performance should meet.

Those interested in incorporating more environmental or sustainability education in their classrooms and schools are fortunate that specific standards exist that will help them craft instruction. The U.S. Partnership for Education for Sustainable Development has created a set of student learning standards for K–12 classrooms. The National Education for Sustainability (EfS) K–12 Learning Standards are freely available for download and are summarized in this appendix (http://k12.uspartnership.org/node/380). Many states also follow the Common Core State Standards (CCSS), which seek to establish uniform learning standards in English language arts, mathematics, and science. These standards are also freely accessible (http://www.corestandards.org). Those that apply to sustainability/environmental studies are summarized in this appendix.

These standards are useful in planning instruction and assessment in the classroom. They are also extremely beneficial when one is working with students who are performing above or below grade level. All students are entitled to an appropriate amount of challenge in the classroom, which entails work that is neither too easy nor to difficult. In the event one or more students in your classroom is performing considerably above or below grade level, the standards are inappropriate. In those cases, it is helpful to look at the standards for lower or higher grades and to use these to increase or decrease the challenge of the instruction based upon students' needs.

Summary of Sustainability Standards Across K–12

	Grades K–4	Grades 5–8	Grades 9–12
1.1 Inter-generational Responsibility	• Family • Generations	• Responsibility to future generations	• Inter-generational equity
2.1 Inter-connectedness	• Relationships • Historical connections • Sense of place	• Systems • Inter-dependency	• Systems thinking • Cradle-to-cradle design
2.2 Ecological Systems	• Connection to nature • Plants, animals, habitats	• Natural resources • Biodiversity • Ecosystems • Ecological footprint • Carrying capacity • Environmental stewardship • Nature as model and teacher	• Respect for limits • Respect for nature • Tragedy of the commons • Environmental justice • Biomimicry • Urban design/land management • Natural capital
2.3 Economic Systems	• Human needs and wants	• Equity • Resource scarcity • Energy economics • Ecological economics • Food systems	• Poverty • Ecosystem services • Alternative indicators and indices of poverty • Globalization • True cost accounting • Triple bottom line • Micro credit

	Grades K–4	Grades 5–8	Grades 9–12
2.4 Social and Cultural Systems	■ Family and friends ■ Personal identity ■ Happiness ■ Fairness ■ Collaborative learning	■ Cultural diversity ■ Multiple perspectives ■ Citizenship ■ Resource distribution ■ Population growth ■ Quality of life indicators ■ Education	■ Human rights ■ Social justice ■ Peace and conflict ■ Multilateral organizations ■ International summits, conferences, conventions and treaties ■ Global health ■ Appropriate technology ■ Governance
3.1 Personal Action	■ Setting goals ■ Communicating ideas ■ Making a difference	■ Personal responsibility ■ Personal footprint calculation ■ Critical thinking ■ Problem solving ■ Project planning and action	■ Accountability ■ Lifelong learning and action ■ Personal change skills and strategies
3.2 Collective Action	■ Setting goals ■ Working together	■ Designing a sustainable system ■ Structural vs. personal solutions ■ Democracy ■ Societal footprint calculation ■ Local, state, and national sustainability plans	■ Local to global responsibility ■ Community-based and societal level decision making ■ Public disclosure and policy ■ Organizational and societal change skills and strategies

Summary of CCSS for English Language Arts/ College and Career Readiness Standards That Support Sustainability/Environmental Studies

	Grades K–5	Grades 6–8	Grades 9–10	Grades 11–12
Key Ideas and Details	CCRA.R.1 CCRA.R.2 CCRA.R.3	RST.6-8.1 RST.6-8.2 RST.6-8.3	RST.9-10.1 RST.9-10.2 RST.9-10.3	RST.11-12.1 RST.11-12.2 RST.11-12.3
Craft and Structure	CCRA.R.4 CCRA.R.5 CCRA.R.6	RST.6-8.4 RST.6-8.5 RST.6-8.6	RST.9-10.4 RST.9-10.5 RST.9-10.6	RST.11-12.4 RST.11-12.5 RST.11-12.6
Integration of Knowledge and Ideas	CCRA.R.7 CCRA.R.8 CCRA.R.9	RST.6-8.7 RST.6-8.8 RST.6-8.9	RST.9-10.7 RST.9-10.8 RST.9-10.9	RST.11-12.7 RST.11-12.8 RST.11-12.9
Range of Reading and Level of Text Complexity	CCRA.R.10	RST.6-8.10	RST.9-10.10	RST.11-12.10
Text Types and Purposes	CCRA.W.1 CCRA.W.2 CCRA.W.3	WHST.6-8.1 WHST.6-8.2 WHST.6-8.3	WHST.9-10.1 WHST.9-10.2	WHST.11-12.1 WHST.11-12.2
Production and Distribution of Writing	CCRA.W.4 CCRA.W.5 CCRA.W.6	WHST.6-8.4 WHST.6-8.5 WHST.6-8.6	WHST.9-10.4 WHST.9-10.5 WHST.9-10.6	WHST.11-12.4 WHST.11-12.5 WHST.11-12.6
Research to Build and Present Writing	CCRA.W.7 CCRA.W.8 CCRA.W.9	WHST.6-8.7 WHST.6-8.8 WHST.6-8.9	WHST.9-10.7 WHST.9-10.8 WHST.9-10.9	WHST.11-12.7 WHST.11-12.8 WHST.11-12.9
Range of Writing	CCRA.W.10	WHST.6-8.10	WHST.9-10.10	WHST.11-12.10
Comprehension and Collaboration	CCRA.SL.1 CCRA.SL.2 CCRA.SL.3	SL.678.1	SL.9-10.1	SL.11-12.1
Presentation of Knowledge and Ideas	CCRA.SL.4 CCRA.SL.5 CCRA.SL.6	SL.678.4 SL.678.5	SL.9-10.4 SL.9-10.5	SL.11-12.4 SL.11-12.5
Vocabulary Acquisition and Use	CCRA.L.4 CCRA.L.5 CCRA.L.6	SL.678.6	SL.9-10.6	SL.11-12.6

About the Authors

Stephen T. Schroth, Ph.D., is a professor of Early Childhood Education and Gifted & Creative Education at Towson University, where he also serves as Graduate Programs Director. Prior to his 15 years in higher education, he served as a classroom teacher, a gifted coordinator, and an arts prototype school coordinator for a decade in the Los Angeles Unified School District. The author of more than 500 publications, including multiple books, monographs, book chapters, and articles, Dr. Schroth holds an M.A. in instructional technology from Teachers College at Columbia University and a Ph.D. in educational psychology/ gifted education from the University of Virginia. Past-Chair of the National Association for Gifted Children (NAGC) Arts Network and the NAGC Conceptual Foundations Network, his research interests include early childhood education, environmental science, differentiated instruction, learning styles, creativity and problem solving, effective instructional and leadership practices, and effective ways of serving English language learners.

Janese Daniels, Ph.D., is a professor of Early Childhood Education at Towson University, where she teaches classes in curriculum, instruction, and technology. Dr. Daniels also serves as Chair of the Department of Early Childhood Education, one of the largest such departments in the United States. Dr. Daniels holds an M.A. in instructional systems development from the University of Maryland,

Baltimore County (UMBC), and a Ph.D. in Education-Human Development from the University of Maryland. A graduate of and former teacher at the Baltimore City Public School System, her work focuses on effective parenting support, new teacher induction, and teacher education.

Common Core State Standards Alignment

Investigation	Subject	Common Core State Standards
1	ELA	CCRA.W.7 Conduct short as well as more sustained research projects based on focused questions, demonstrating understanding of the subject under investigation.
2	ELA	CCRA.W.2 Write informative/explanatory texts to examine and convey complex ideas and information clearly and accurately through the effective selection, organization, and analysis of content.
	Math	1.NBT.B Understand place value.
3	Math	K.MD.B Classify objects and count the number of objects in each category.
		1.MD.A Measure lengths indirectly and by iterating length units.
4	Math	2.G.A Reason with shapes and their attributes.
5	Math	2.OA.B Add and subtract within 20.
6	Math	2.MD.D Represent and interpret data.
7	Math	2.OA.C Work with equal groups of objects to gain foundations for multiplication.

Investigation	Subject	Common Core State Standards
8	ELA	CCRA.W.8 Gather relevant information from multiple print and digital sources, assess the credibility and accuracy of each source, and integrate the information while avoiding plagiarism.
		CCRA.SL.1 Prepare for and participate effectively in a range of conversations and collaborations with diverse partners, building on others' ideas and expressing their own clearly and persuasively.
		CCRA.SL.4 Present information, findings, and supporting evidence such that listeners can follow the line of reasoning and the organization, development, and style are appropriate to task, purpose, and audience.
		CCRA.SL.5 Make strategic use of digital media and visual displays of data to express information and enhance understanding of presentations.
		CCRA.SL.6 Adapt speech to a variety of contexts and communicative tasks, demonstrating command of formal English when indicated or appropriate.
	Math	2.MD.D Represent and interpret data.
9	ELA	CCRA.R.1 Read closely to determine what the text says explicitly and to make logical inferences from it; cite specific textual evidence when writing or speaking to support conclusions drawn from the text.
		CCRA.R.2 Determine central ideas or themes of a text and analyze their development; summarize the key supporting details and ideas.
		CCRA.R.3 Analyze how and why individuals, events, or ideas develop and interact over the course of a text.
		CCRA.R.5 Analyze the structure of texts, including how specific sentences, paragraphs, and larger portions of the text (e.g., a section, chapter, scene, or stanza) relate to each other and the whole.

Investigation	Subject	Common Core State Standards
9, *continued*	ELA, *continued*	CCRA.W.1 Write arguments to support claims in an analysis of substantive topics or texts using valid reasoning and relevant and sufficient evidence.
		CCRA.W.2 Write informative/explanatory texts to examine and convey complex ideas and information clearly and accurately through the effective selection, organization, and analysis of content.
		CCRA.W.5 Develop and strengthen writing as needed by planning, revising, editing, rewriting, or trying a new approach.
		CCRA.W.6 Use technology, including the Internet, to produce and publish writing and to interact and collaborate with others.
		CCRA.W.7 Conduct short as well as more sustained research projects based on focused questions, demonstrating understanding of the subject under investigation.
		CCRA.W.8 Gather relevant information from multiple print and digital sources, assess the credibility and accuracy of each source, and integrate the information while avoiding plagiarism.
		CCRA.SL.2 Integrate and evaluate information presented in diverse media and formats, including visually, quantitatively, and orally.
		CCRA.SL.6 Adapt speech to a variety of contexts and communicative tasks, demonstrating command of formal English when indicated or appropriate.
		CCRA.L.1 Demonstrate command of the conventions of standard English grammar and usage when writing or speaking.
		CCRA.L.2 Demonstrate command of the conventions of standard English capitalization, punctuation, and spelling when writing.

Investigation	Subject	Common Core State Standards
10	ELA	CCRA.W.1 Write arguments to support claims in an analysis of substantive topics or texts using valid reasoning and relevant and sufficient evidence.
		CCRA.W.2 Write informative/explanatory texts to examine and convey complex ideas and information clearly and accurately through the effective selection, organization, and analysis of content.
		CCRA.W.3 Write narratives to develop real or imagined experiences or events using effective technique, well-chosen details and well-structured event sequences.W.2.8 Recall information from experiences or gather information from provided sources to answer a question.
		CCRA.W.8 Gather relevant information from multiple print and digital sources, assess the credibility and accuracy of each source, and integrate the information while avoiding plagiarism.
		CCRA.SL.4 Present information, findings, and supporting evidence such that listeners can follow the line of reasoning and the organization, development, and style are appropriate to task, purpose, and audience.
		CCRA.SL.5 Make strategic use of digital media and visual displays of data to express information and enhance understanding of presentations.
		CCRA.SL.6 Adapt speech to a variety of contexts and communicative tasks, demonstrating command of formal English when indicated or appropriate.

*For Product Safety Concerns and Information please contact
our EU representative GPSR@taylorandfrancis.com Taylor & Francis
Verlag GmbH, Kaufingerstraße 24, 80331 München, Germany*

T - #0076 - 090625 - C0 - 280/210/9 - PB - 9781646320585 - Gloss Lamination